OUTLIER INVESTORS

What Successful Investors Do
(That Everyone Else Doesn't)

ISBN 978-1-7359229-2-8 (paperback)
ISBN 978-1-7359229-3-5 (eBook)

Contact Information
Inquires related to publishing rights, translation deals, and media appearances should be submitted to danial.jiwani@danialjiwani.com

Disclaimer
Outlier Investors, Danial Jiwani, and his companies and affiliates ("The Entities") are not an investment advisory service, a registered investment advisor or a broker-dealer and do not undertake to advise clients on which securities they should buy or sell for themselves. It must be understood that investing can involve significant risks. The Entities do not assume responsibility or liability for investment results. The Entities provide information for educational purposes only, which should not be construed as investment advice. Investors and traders must always consult with their licensed financial advisor and tax professional to determine the suitability of any investment.

Position Disclaimers
Danial Jiwani has long positions in the following securities that are mentioned in *Outlier Investors*: Apple (AAPL), Amazon (AMZN), Facebook (FB), and General Electric (GE).

OUTLIER INVESTORS

What Successful Investors Do
(That Everyone Else Doesn't)

by Danial Jiwani

out·li·er

out ˌlīər

1. a person or thing situated away or detached from the main body or system
2. a person or thing differing from all other members of a particular group or set

in·vest·or

in ˈvestər

1. a person or organization that puts money into financial plans, property, etc. with the expectation of achieving a profit.

Contents

An Introduction to *Outlier Investors*

· ·

During my sophomore year of high school, when I first got into investing, I was looking for my first stock to buy. At the time, I didn't have a method for screening stocks, so I would just read articles online to generate investment ideas.

One of the articles said that a company called General Electric was a sound investment for two reasons. First, its stock was down. General Electric had been trading at $250, but a year later, was at $190. The stock price's decline created a good "buy low, sell high" opportunity, according to the article. Second, General Electric was a great company. It was a large blue-chip company that was doing over $100 billion in sales. The company had been around for over 100 years. So, it must be a safe investment.

I decided to buy some shares in General Electric at $190.48.

Afterwards, the stock went down a little bit to $180. "No worries," I told myself. The stock will probably come back up soon.

The stock then went to $140. "The markets are probably being a little bit emotional," I reassured myself.

Then the price dropped to $100. "Just be greedy when others are fearful."

Then it fell to $60. "Maybe I don't really know what I'm doing."

With the money that I didn't invest in General Electric, I decided to buy some books about investing so that I could learn about it.

The introductions of many of those books made big promises.

Some of them said that investing is easy. They would say, "People think picking stocks is really difficult. In reality, it's not. All you must do is follow my simple strategy and buy large brand-name companies that have low P/E ratios and high margins."

And some of them would say that investing only requires a small time commitment. "Back in the day, investing required a lot of work. Investors didn't have computers, so they had to manually screen hundreds of stocks. Today, however, we have stock screeners that can create a shortlist of the most attractive investment opportunities. All you must do is just conduct a little due diligence on the ones you want to buy. And voilà! You'll outperform the S&P 500."

At first, I believed those claims. If you read several books that claim that investing is easy, if you come across ads that claim that investing doesn't require much work, and if you come across media authorities that claim that you can easily replicate Warren Buffett's success, those ideas gain social proof. So, you start to believe them. "If everyone says investing is easy, how could it be hard?"

But over time, I learned that investing is not as easy as people say it is. Just think about it. The stock market is filled with thousands and thousands of investors. Those investors are constantly monitoring the markets. Many of them have had decades of experience in picking stocks. They may even be spending many more hours than you hunting for undervalued stocks. That means, to truly do well at investing, you have to be better than them—the highly competitive Wall Street professionals. If you aren't, they will identify the best investment opportunities before you do, and they will leave you in the dust. As my college professor, Mr. Excell, once told the class, "outperforming the markets isn't easy because there is so much competition."

Despite the challenge of investing, many information sources—influencers, media outlets, websites, and books—claim that investing is so easy because it helps achieve business objectives.

Just think about it.

No one is going to click on a website that says, "Investing is Very Difficult and Time-Consuming." That's not an appealing story. What makes media companies money is a story that says, "How I Outperformed Warren Buffett Last Year by Following One Trading Pattern." People are going to click on that.

No one is going to buy an influencer's course if their pitch is, "good investing requires a decent time commitment." What sells is, "I have a formula that doubled my money last year."

The same thing happens in the book publishing industry, but more subtly. Readers are attracted to investment books with "simple strategies" and promises to "easily outperform the market." For authors, then, it makes perfect sense to present the reader with a "get rich quick" strategy. Doing so makes the reader happy, leading to positive book reviews and increased sales.

However, those books don't necessarily provide the insights that you need to succeed. They often contain a watered-down investment philosophy because the author only wants to present ideas that are simple and easy to implement. That's what sells, after all.

Of course, that's not good for the reader; learning watered-down information doesn't improve one's ability to make investment decisions. Moreover, since many investment practices that improve decision-making require the reader to make an effort to implement them, some books don't talk about them. Those writers want to keep things simple, so they sometimes don't share the information you need to succeed.

This book, however, will not provide a watered-down investment framework. It will not oversimply information for the sake of sales. Instead, it aims to be as transparent as possible. If an investment insight is simple to implement but won't truly improve your investment abilities, I won't share it. If an investment insight can greatly improve your ability to pick stocks but requires some effort on your end, I will still share it—even if it hurts reviews. If investing is difficult, this book will clearly say so. That's what I believe is right for you, and that is what I believe is the right thing to do.

THE PURPOSE OF THIS BOOK

Most investors don't consistently outperform the market.

That's not just true for retail investors. It's also true for professional investors.

According to CNBC, about 85% of large cap, actively managed funds underperformed the market over a 10 year period.

In fact, that's a statistic most investors are aware of.

Yet, they still attempt to outperform the market because they believe that they are in the minority of investors who can do so.

They often believe that they are in the minority because they have studied the strategies of investors who have outperformed the market, like Warren Buffett. For example, many of these investors read well-known books like *The Intelligent Investor,* watch recordings of speeches by world-renowned investors like Peter Lynch, Ray Dalio, and Mohnish Pabrai, and attempt to understand the fundamentals of Buffett's investment philosophy. After all, "surely studying the lessons of the greatest investors should allow me to replicate their successes."

But most investors fail to replicate the successes of the Buffetts of the world.

Consider this. I looked at the performance of several major investment funds. All of these funds' investment philosophies are based on Buffett's. In fact, several of these funds have a reputation for only hiring individuals who have read every page of *The Intelligent Investor* and every sentence of Buffett's letters to shareholders.

What you generally find is that they underperform—just like everyone else. And if they outperform, they don't do so significantly after fees.

Fund A, for example, is a concentrated fund. That means that they reduce diversification to put more money into their best investment ideas, allowing them to maximize returns. Fund A also has a reputation for only hiring people who are committed students of Warren Buffett's investment philosophy.

They have underperformed—before considering fees. Before big fees, they earned an annualized 12.29% return over the past 10 years, whereas the S&P 500 (the benchmark in the finance industry) earned 12.96% over the same period.

Or consider Fund B. It is a very well known "value fund," and, just like Fund A, is a concentrated fund. Moreover, in the investment industry, they are known for attracting the best followers of Buffett. In fact, I know of several people who have stated that their dream job was to work at this firm. Yet, all their non-international funds have underperformed the market. Before large fees, their best performing non-international fund returned 10.70% over the past ten years, whereas the S&P 500 returned 12.96%.

These examples are not anomalies. There are many other funds just like them. In the following graph, I have listed the performance of several other major investment firms. These firms market themselves as having an investment philosophy like that of Buffett. And as you can see, they haven't outperformed the S&P 500 materially.

Many followers of Warren Buffett underperform the S&P 500

% return (before fees) over the 10 years before Q2 2022

Sources omitted to protect brand names of the funds

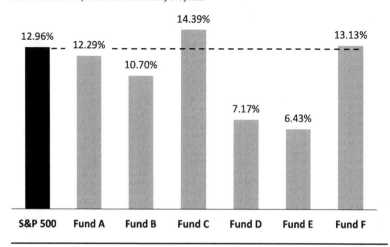

A logical conclusion from these data points would be that it is impossible to outperform the market. This is the claim of people who support efficient market theory—the finance theory that essentially states that it is impossible to identify undervalued stocks and outperform the market.

On the surface, that conclusion is not illogical at all. There are simply too many datapoints that indicate that it is nearly impossible to outperform the market. Most professional investors underperform the market. Even many followers of Buffett underperform. "If everyone underperforms, including professional practitioners of Buffett's philosophy, surely it must be impossible to outperform."

However, there are some Outliers. Some investors, Outlier Investors, are able to consistently outperform the market. Lou Simpson is one of these Outliers. In 1979, Warren Buffett hired Lou Simpson as a portfolio manager for GEICO. Lou Simpson went on to develop a phenomenal track record. From 1980 to 2004, Lou Simpson earned 20.3% per year, whereas the S&P 500 earned 13.5% per year. In other words, he outperformed the S&P 500 by almost 7% per year. Moreover, that level of outperformance spanned more than two decades, which is a statistically significant track record.

Or consider Berkshire Hathaway, the company that Buffett started. From 1964-2021, Berkshire Hathaway had an overall gain of 3,641,613%, whereas the S&P 500 returned only 30,209%. Warren Buffett and Charlie Munger have had most of their net worth in Berkshire Hathaway during that time frame, allowing both to outperform the market.

Another example is Peter Lynch, who ran Fidelity's Magellan Fund for 13 years. During that period, he earned 29.2% per year, more than twice the return of the S&P 500.

Therefore, it wouldn't be fair to say that it is impossible to outperform the market consistently. There are Outliers—Lou Simpson, Warren Buffett, and Peter Lynch—who can consistently outperform the market.

To outperform the market, the Buffetts of the world do things differently from everyone else. For example, many prominent investors—Buffett, Simpson, Bill Ackman, Mohnish Pabrai, and Peter Lynch—believe that most investors overdiversify. Hence, they advocate for owning a concentrated portfolio of stocks. Most notably, Warren Buffett has said that he would be perfectly comfortable only owning three stocks in his portfolio. That would allow him to concentrate his money on the best ideas, increasing his long-term returns. That's a different philosophy from many investors, who aim to have a diversified portfolio that's exposed to every sector and industry.

Another thing that Outlier Investors are known for doing differently is differentiating between volatility and risk. Some people, particularly in academia, say that volatility (how much a stock moves up and down in price) determines the risk of the stock. In simple terms, they would say that more volatile stocks have more uncertainty because the more a stock's price moves, the wider the range of potential outcomes; if the price moves a lot, it can go up a lot, but it can also go down a lot. Hence, they would say that volatility equates to risk. However, Outlier Investors think differently. Investors like Buffett and Lynch argue that risk shouldn't be measured by volatility. Instead, they say that it should be measured by business risk—the risk that the company's competitive strength will weaken.

To learn more about what successful investors do differently from everyone else, most people read many of the mainstream books on investing: *The Intelligent Investor, Rule #1 Investing, One Up on Wall Street, The Dhandho Investor*, etc. "After all, if I know every detail of how successful investors outperform, it wouldn't be difficult for me to outperform as well. If I read Lynch's book *One Up on Wall Street* and the book that shaped Buffett's investment philosophy, *The Intelligent Investor*, surely I should be able to outperform like them."

But that doesn't happen. Most investors have read many of those books. Yet, as the data indicates, they still don't materially outperform. They sometimes outperform by a percent or two, but they don't even come close to the level of outperformance of people like Buffett and Lynch.

The fact that many investors don't outperform—even after reading all the mainstream investment books—tells me that every important investment idea hasn't been written down yet. If all the keys to outperforming were written down in those books, outperforming would be as simple as just applying the lessons from those books. But, as we know, most investors don't outperform after simply reading them.

That brings me to the purpose of this book. My goal for this book is to help explain what successful investors do (that everyone else doesn't). In particular, it's to explain things that Outlier Investors do differently from everyone else that haven't been deeply covered by mainstream investment books.

Will I cover everything that successful investors do (that everyone else doesn't)? Probably not.

It is not possible to learn everything about the way Outlier Investors think differently. Rightfully, many successful investors don't like to share everything they know. For example, Buffett was recently asked why his investment managers, Ted Welcher and Todd Combs, don't publicly appear at the Berkshire Hathaway annual meetings. In response, Buffett said that he doesn't want them teaching everyone about picking stocks:

> [Ted Welcher and Todd Combs] are both absolutely terrific. And that's one reason. I don't want people quizzing them on stocks... There's no reason for them to be out educating other people on how to compete with us.

So, even if I researched everything the Buffetts of the world have ever written or said, I likely wouldn't come across every little detail on investing.

Will this book share a magic formula that will allow you to pick the next homerun with just 15 minutes of effort? Definitely not. As mentioned earlier, good investing requires more than just a little effort. If it were that easy, almost every actively managed fund wouldn't underperform.

But what this book can do is significantly improve your ability to make intelligent investment decisions. It breaks down at least some of the things that successful investors do (that everyone else doesn't).

Chapter 1 explains why Charlie Munger says that he doesn't "understand" simple businesses like Apple and why Warren Buffett says that he doesn't understand Hochschild-Kohn (a simple department store).

Chapter 2 teaches you how Nick Sleep "built his second layer of competence" to identify that Amazon would change the world while it was still in its early stages (and how he became comfortable concentrating 70% of his net worth into Amazon, allowing him to earn 900%+ returns for his fund).

Chapter 3 explains why closely studying what's going on in the markets is potentially a backward investment approach.

Chapter 4 highlights why Outlier Investors don't merely read annual reports, industry reports, and earnings transcripts to research stocks (and what they do instead).

Chapter 5 reveals why a "margin of safety" is rarely adequate for mitigating risk.

Chapter 6 explains why conducting thorough due diligence rarely uncovers the risks of an investment.

Chapter 7 explains why Warren Buffett oftentimes ignores macroeconomic information (and what he pays attention to instead).

Chapter 8 shares how I learned that a good resume doesn't need to have "a lot of numbers and active verbs" (and what that taught me about how Outlier Investors form contrarian opinions on the market).

Chapter 9 reveals what allows Warren Buffett to claim that he can make investment decisions "within [just] 5 minutes" (and how you can apply the same technique when investing).

In short, this book brings you one step closer to becoming an Outlier.

HOW OUTLIERS EVALUATE REWARD

· ·

No One Understands Coca-Cola

Charlie Munger, who co-founded Berkshire Hathaway with Warren Buffett, was at the 2019 annual shareholders' meeting for The Daily Journal, as he was the chairman of the company.

During the meeting, an avid investor asked Munger whether Berkshire Hathaway was likely to invest more money in Apple, in which it already had a large stake.

In response, you would have expected Munger to give one of two answers: either, "We think that it is a great time to buy Apple stock, so we will continue to buy more," or, "We don't want to buy more shares because it's not a good buying opportunity."

But Munger didn't give either answer.

Instead, he shocked some investors by saying that he didn't understand Apple:

> I'm a very opinionated man, and I know a lot. But I don't know everything. I like Apple, but I don't have the feeling that I'm the big expert [on Apple].

Of course, it is always important to invest in companies that you understand. Peter Lynch, an Outlier Investor who returned over 29% per year for 13 years, famously said, "know what you own and know why you own it." The reason he said that is simple; if you start investing in biotech and semiconductor companies that you don't understand, you are going to lose money. In that case, you aren't going to accurately assess whether the business will be successful in the long-term. The same isn't true with a business that you understand. Take Kraft Heinz, the company that makes Ketchup, as an example. It's fairly easy to understand Kraft Heinz's business model and understand that it has competitive products. Unlike how you might not even know whether a biotech company will be in business tomorrow, you can be reasonably certain that Kraft Heinz will sell Ketchup tomorrow. Therefore, you will be far more accurate when attempting to predict whether Kraft Heinz's business will be successful than whether a biotech company will be successful.

But Munger's response raises an important question: why didn't he say that he understood Apple?

It would make sense if he said he didn't understand bitcoin.

And it would make sense if he said he didn't understand a biotech start-up.

But why Apple?

Apple has very simple products. I don't think anyone would have any confusion over what an iPhone is.

Apple's competitive positioning is also straightforward. I don't think many people would question whether Apple has a dominant brand and product.

Apple's business doesn't fluctuate dramatically. While a start-up might be blowing up one day and crashing the next, Apple has a long, consistent history of producing profits.

And remember, Munger didn't make that statement in the early 2000s, when the iPhone was new. He made it in 2019, once Apple had clearly asserted its competitive positioning.

What many people don't realize is that very simple businesses can actually be quite difficult to understand.

Coca-Cola is the perfect example of this.

By most people's standards, Coca-Cola is a very simple

business to understand. Most people understand what Coca-Cola sells, whom they sell cola to, who the main competitors are, and many other factors.

But what many people don't realize is that they don't have a strong understanding of Coca-Cola. In particular, many people don't thoroughly understand why Coca-Cola is more competitive than Pepsi. How do I know? Well, I've asked people why they believe Coca-Cola is stronger than Pepsi. In response, they almost always cite incorrect reasons.

A common reason why investors buy Coca-Cola's stock is that it has a phenomenal product. There is no question that it is a good product. It tastes good. It's addictive. It's refreshing. It has all the qualities that people want in their drinks (except for the fact that it isn't healthy).

But it would be a mistake to say that Coca-Cola is stronger than Pepsi due to having a better product. Objectively, Coca-Cola doesn't have a better product than Pepsi. In fact, many consumers can't even taste the difference between Pepsi and Coca-Cola. Don't take it from me. Instead, take it from research. A group of researchers ran a blind taste test, where they asked individuals to drink various cola brands like Coca-Cola and Pepsi. Since it was a blind taste test, the participants didn't know what brands of cola they were actually drinking. Once the participants drank the cola, the researchers asked them, "what drink did you just have?" In response, the participants couldn't tell what drink they had actually had. When the participants were given Pepsi, 55% thought they were having Coca-Cola or another drink. When the participants were given Coca-Cola, 41% told the researchers that they thought they were drinking Pepsi. Therefore, it would be a mistake to conclude that Coca-Cola tastes much better than Pepsi. To most consumers, they don't even taste very different.

Other investors say that Coca-Cola is more competitive than Pepsi because Coca-Cola has higher customer loyalty. For example, one famous "value investor" (whom I'll leave anonymous) once said that what makes Coca-Cola a "powerful brand" is that its customers are "fanatically loyal," which makes it "very hard to get [customers] to switch." But the truth is that the majority of Coca-Cola customers aren't "fanatically loyal" fans who are "very hard" to convince to "switch." Just look at the data. TNS conducted a study on the brand loyalty of Coca-Cola drinkers. Did they find that Coca-Cola drinkers were "fanatically loyal" and "hard to convince to drink Pepsi?" Not at all. They found the exact opposite. According to the study, 72% of Coca-Cola drinkers also drank Pepsi during their analysis period. Therefore, it would be a mistake to conclude that Coca-Cola is more competitive than Pepsi because it has developed a highly loyal customer base that locks in customers. It hasn't. If anything, Coca-Cola's customer base is often disloyal and chooses to use its competitors' products.

Coca-Cola drinkers aren't loyal to Coca-Cola; they also drink competing brands like Pepsi

Percent (%) of buyers who also purchased regular Coca-Cola during analysis period

Source: TNS data from "How Brands Grow"

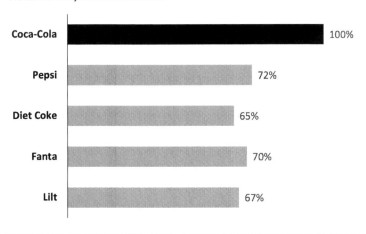

Some investors, then, say that Coca-Cola positions its brand differently from its competitors. After all, "why else would Coca-Cola spend billions of dollars on advertising every year? Surely it doesn't want to position itself in the same manner as Pepsi." But once again, the data says otherwise. World-class market researcher Byron Sharp wanted to understand whether buyers perceived brands as being differentiated from the competition, so he simply asked consumers whether they perceived various cola brands as being different and unique. In response, consumers largely reported that they didn't perceive that they were very different. For example, only 8% of consumers reported that they thought Coca-Cola's brand was different from its competitors' brands, and only 13% of consumers reported that they thought Coca-Cola's brand was unique compared to its competitors' brands.

Coca-Cola's brand isn't positioned differently from competitors

Brand	Different	Unique	Either
Coca-Cola	8%	13%	19%
Diet Coke	9%	8%	15%
Pepsi	7%	10%	15%
Fanta	8%	5%	12%
Canada Dry	10%	9%	17%

If you think about it, these results make sense. Why? Well, because Coca-Cola and Pepsi position their brands in a similar manner.

Coca-Cola tries to convince consumers that its beverages are refreshing drinks that will make them happy. Consider Coca-Cola's "Open that Coca-Cola" ad campaign. The advertisement shows several groups of people doing ordinary things: shopping for groceries, playing video games, eating dinner, and watching a soccer game. Initially, the scene is dull, with everything looking normal. Suddenly, the people drink a sip of Coca-Cola, which causes everyone to start dancing with large smiles on their faces. What's that ad communicating? Coca-Cola takes people from feeling alright to feeling extremely happy.

Pepsi tries to convince consumers of the exact same thing. Consider the 2003 Pepsi ad called "Crazy in Love." The ad is simple. It shows Beyoncé getting out of her car to get a can of Pepsi. After taking a sip, she gives a big smile and looks at the camera. After a brief encounter with a man, Beyoncé walks back to her car while the song "Crazy in Love" plays in the background. The ad ends with the scene cutting to a black screen with the phrase "The Joy of Pepsi" written in the center. Is this ad not also communicating that Pepsi will make consumers happy? The "Joy" of Pepsi, Beyoncé's big smile, and the upbeat music all communicate that Pepsi is a source of happiness.

So, why is Coca-Cola actually competitive? What makes it stronger than Pepsi? (That, by the way, is a question most investors can't answer correctly).

Well, the reason is that Coca-Cola is more strongly associated with happiness than Pepsi.

People always buy products to solve problems. People buy Netflix subscriptions to get rid of boredom. People buy books to increase their knowledge. Similarly, people buy sugary beverages to solve a problem. But that problem isn't only thirst. If it were, then people would just buy water because it is the cheapest way to quench their thirst. Instead, people choose to pay more for sugary beverages because they solve an additional problem. They make people happier than water does.

When it comes to consumer products, people tend to buy the products that most easily come to the tops of their minds as a solution. Cinnamon Toast Crunch is a perfect example. In every Cinnamon Toast Crunch commercial, for example, you see the "Crazy Squares" happily cannibalizing on fellow Cinnamon Toast. That story line memorably communicates that Cinnamon Toast Crunch is a tasty cereal. In effect, consumers end up remembering that Cinnamon Toast Crunch tastes great when they are shopping for cereal. That makes it more likely that an individual will choose Cinnamon Toast Crunch over a competing product.

Both Coca-Cola and Pepsi do the exact same thing. Both companies try to memorably communicate that their beverages will make consumers feel refreshed and happy. Doing so increases the chance that consumers will recall that those drinks will actually make them feel happy and refreshed in a buying situation, which increases the chances of consumers purchasing them.

However, Coca-Cola has been significantly more effective than Pepsi at communicating that message. For one thing, Coca-Cola had a head start. The first glass of Coca-Cola was sold in 1886, whereas Pepsi was founded in 1965. That gave Coca-Cola over 50 years to establish its brand as the one that "makes [people] smile," allowing Coca-Cola to assert itself without significant competition. Moreover, Coca-Cola can spend more money on marketing than Pepsi. Consider that in recent years, Coca-Cola has spent roughly $4 billion per year in advertising, whereas PepsiCo has spent roughly $5 billion per year in advertising. Although PepsiCo spends more money on ads, it is important to keep in mind that PepsiCo has a wider range of brands. Whereas Coca-Cola mainly operates in the beverage industry, PepsiCo is more diversified in other areas. Most notably, it owns Frito-Lay and Quaker Oats. What that means is that PepsiCo's $5 billion advertising budget is more thinly spread across all its brands, whereas Coca-Cola's is more concentrated on the Coca-Cola brand. Therefore, the

Coca-Cola beverage has likely been receiving more advertising support than the Pepsi brand. That allows Coca-Cola to more frequently communicate its brand message to customers.

"I UNDERSTAND THE BUSINESS. IT'S SIMPLE."

The reason I took you through that long explanation of Coca-Cola and Pepsi is to thoroughly illustrate a point. A business can be simple. But the fact that a business is simple doesn't mean that you understand it.

Coca-Cola has by far the simplest business model in the world. It's so simple that a 4-year-old would be able to explain how it makes money. I could ask virtually any investor in the world whether they understand Coca-Cola's business, and they would all say yes.

But the reality is that they don't understand Coca-Cola. As previously illustrated, people often cite the wrong reasons why Coca-Cola is stronger than Pepsi. They say that "Coca-Cola is stronger than Pepsi because it tastes better and because it has a differentiated brand." But as we know, those reasons aren't accurate. Even if they don't cite those incorrect reasons, they can rarely cite the right reason why Coca-Cola is stronger than Pepsi; they rarely recognize that Coca-Cola is more closely associated with happiness than Pepsi.

You might be wondering, "why is it so important for me to know that Coca-Cola is associated with happiness?"

Charlie Munger and Warren Buffett have frequently said that the reason they outperform and everyone else underperforms is that they know the edge of their own competency, while others don't. And the Coca-Cola example vividly illustrates that most people don't know the edge of their competency.

Imagine someone investing in Amazon without knowing that they offer 2-day shipping, affordable prices, and wide product selection. You would conclude that they don't understand Amazon because they don't understand why it is competitive.

Or imagine someone investing in Apple without knowing that the iPhone is better designed than competing phones. You would conclude that they don't have a basic understanding of why Apple is competitive.

It's the same thing for Coca-Cola. If someone invests in Coca-Cola without understanding that it is associated with happiness, they probably don't understand why it is truly competitive. (That person probably doesn't understand brands in the first place, because a brand's reputation matters). In fact, Coca-Cola's association with happiness is part of why Buffett invested in it in the first place:

> Coca-Cola will sell a billion and a half eight-ounce servings of its product around the world today. There is something in every person's mind virtually in the globe about Coca-Cola. That product, since 1886, has been associated with happiness and good value in terms of refreshment... It's just about impossible... to take on a product like that.

Recognizing that simple businesses aren't necessarily understandable has helped me stay within my circle of competence, as Warren Buffett would say.[1]

Not very long ago, I was analyzing a company that sold shoes. By all means, it was a very simple business. It simply sold shoes through retail and e-commerce. A business doesn't get much simpler than that.

Yet I couldn't understand why it was competitive. I noticed that the company had a significantly larger market share than most of its peers. But I couldn't figure out why. Its competitors had a

---

1   For those who are new to investing, the phrase 'staying within your circle of competence' means to only invest in companies that you understand. Conversely, 'stepping outside of your circle of competence' means that one has invested in a business that they don't understand. The term circle of competence was popularized by Warren Buffett, and will be used several times throughout the book.

very similar business model. It had the same sales per square foot as its major competitors. It had similar margins as competitors. So I couldn't find anything that the company was doing better than competitors. Just as how Coca-Cola being associated with happiness makes it competitive, I couldn't merely identify what exactly made the business stronger than its competitors; I didn't know what drove the company's competitiveness. More importantly, I couldn't understand how those drivers would impact the company's competitiveness in the future. So, I had to face reality and admit to myself that I didn't understand the business.

By all means, it was a simple business. But it didn't mean that I understood it.

Some of Warren Buffett's mistakes were caused by thinking that "simple businesses" are "understandable businesses."

In their early days, Warren Buffett, Charlie Munger, and Sandy Gottesman, a current board member of Berkshire Hathaway, created a holding company called Diversified Retailing. Buffett owned 80%, Munger owned 10%, and Gottesman owned 10%. They intended to use Diversified Retailing to purchase retail businesses.

The first company they decided to buy was a department store called Hochschild-Kohn. The business was trading at a great price. As Warren Buffett recounts, "we were buying a second-class department store at a third-class price." On top of that, they thought that they could easily understand the business. "How much simpler could a business get? The competitive landscape is simple because the only competitors are nearby stores. I use and know of many of the products the company sells. How hard could it be to understand a department store?"

Apparently, it's quite hard. The business was simple. But it was hard to understand it. In particular, Buffett and Munger didn't understand the competitive environment. They overlooked how threatening the competition would be. In Munger's own words, "we didn't weigh heavily enough the intense competition between four different department stores in Baltimore at a time when department stores no longer had an automatic edge."

On top of that, they simply didn't understand anything about retailing. As Alice Schroeder mentions in the Snowball Effect, "Within the first couple of years at Hochschild-Kohn, Buffett had figured out that the essential skill in retailing was merchandising, not finance."

In the end, the investment didn't turn out well. Buffett and Munger realized that it was a mistake. They concluded that it was best to sell Hochschild-Kohn. So, they ended up selling it for about the price they had paid for it initially, earning a roughly 0% return on investment.

The Hochschild-Kohn investment mistake could have been prevented if Buffett and Munger had recognized the difference between a simple business and an understandable one. If they realized that a business can be simple but not understandable, then they would have realized that they don't necessarily understand Hochschild-Kohn because it is simple. In that case, they would have been careful not to step outside of their circles of competence.

But don't take that lesson from me. Take it from Warren Buffett. During a recent annual meeting, Buffett spoke about the cause of the Hochschild-Kohn failure. What did he say caused the investment to go sour? According to him, the investment failed because he assumed that the business was understandable because it was also simple:

> Charlie and I have been reasonably good at identifying what I would call the perimeter of my circle of competence. But, obviously, we have gone out of it. In my own case, I've gone out of it more often in retail than in any other arena. I think it is easy to sort of think that you understand retail and subsequently...find out you don't, as we did with a department store in Baltimore [Hochschild-Kohn].

Therefore, never assume that a simple business is understandable.

Buffett recognized that Hochschild-Kohn was a simple business. But, in hindsight, he realized that he didn't understand it.

Charlie Munger knows that Apple is a simple business. But it doesn't mean that he understands it.

And most investors know that Coca-Cola is a simple business. But that doesn't mean that they understand it.

After reading this section, many readers are left with important questions in their minds. "If I don't understand Coca-Cola, what do I understand? How can I identify whether I actually understand a simple business?" Don't worry. All your questions will be answered. But first, I'm going to cover two more scenarios where investors think that they understand a business, when they really don't.

"I KNOW THE PRODUCT, I KNOW THE STOCK"

According to Social Categorization Theory, we like to group individuals into categories based on various characteristics. For example, let's say that you come across an individual with the following characteristics: they smell bad, aren't well dressed, and are begging for money. Your mind will automatically categorize that individual as being homeless. The homeless individual wouldn't have to tell you that they are homeless for you to recognize that they are homeless. Your mind can automatically infer that because they do not have a tidy appearance and are asking for money. Similarly, if you come across a person on a basketball court shooting a basketball, you will naturally infer that they are a basketball player.

We categorize individuals as being part of groups because it conserves energy. Just imagine having to ask someone whether they are homeless every time an individual asked you for money at a red light. That wouldn't be an efficient way to go about life. Or imagine having to ask someone with a basketball on a basketball court, "do you play basketball" to learn whether they do. That would also be a waste of time because you could safely assume that they play basketball.

However, the downside of social categorization is that we may mis-categorize things. Let's say that at 8:00 am, you come across an individual with a flashy watch, and they are walking into Goldman Sachs's headquarters. Your mind will use that information to infer that they are a highly successful working professional. After all, they have a fancy outfit, and they are walking into one of the most prestigious financial firms. In reality, that conclusion might be totally incorrect. Instead, they might not be very successful, but they are going into Goldman Sachs's headquarters because a family friend was able to get them a job interview.

Just as you use mental shortcuts to draw inferences about people, you use mental shortcuts to draw inferences about stocks. In particular, you use rules of thumb to decide whether a business is within your circle of competence.

For example, people have a rule of thumb that says, "I understand a business if I use its products." They like to categorize stocks as being within their circle of competence because they use a company's products. This is just like how you might categorize an individual as a successful professional because they are walking into Goldman Sachs's office. Or it's like how you might categorize a stock as being within your circle of competence because the business is simple.

On the surface, it sounds logical to say that "you understand a business if you use its products." All else equal, you will understand the competitive dynamics of a business better if you are its customer. Being a consumer of a product allows you to gain some insight into what the customer cares about. Moreover, it allows you to easily understand who the leaders and laggards are in any market.

However, it isn't always a good rule of thumb to rely on. Just as it can be incorrect to assume that someone has a successful career because they are walking into Goldman Sachs, it can be very incorrect to assume that you understand a business because you use the company's products.

Take the example of one investor. I knew of an individual who once said something among the lines of, "GoPro is a great company. I've bought two GoPros. The camera quality is fantastic. Everyone is going to love the product. It's simply better than the competition. GoPro just had its IPO, so let me buy shares in the company before Wall Street figures out how great of a product GoPro has."

Despite his high hopes, the investment went sour.

In just a few quarters, sales growth turned negative, and consumers stopped showing signs of liking GoPro's products.

GoPro was confident that its newest camera, the Hero4 Session, would go viral like its previous products, so it didn't dedicate a significant marketing budget to it. But it didn't go viral like GoPro's previous products.

Moreover, GoPro overestimated how much consumers would love the product. GoPro CEO Nick Woodman thought that his newest product was "the ultimate GoPro." So, Woodman priced it like a premium product at $400 per camera. But consumers didn't perceive it to be a premium product, and sales weren't coming in. So, Woodman had to cut its price by $200 or 50%.

Even worse, the GoPro investor overlooked a big risk: Apple. Soon after GoPro's initial public offering, consumers started to realize the benefits of using Apple's camera. In particular, they realized that it was far more convenient to simply use their iPhone's high-quality camera than to carry an extra camera around. "I'm already carrying a phone that has a camera, so why do I need to bring another camera with me? After all, the cameras are reasonably similar in terms of quality." As one critic of GoPro said:

> Do most GoPro products get used by athletes and scuba divers? Based on the number of cameras it sells, probably not. The fact that the media that follow Apple (Nasdaq: AAPL) would even make a comparison between an iPhone 6s and a GoPro Hero 4 is damaging all by itself.... With the launch of the iPhone 7 just months away, the odds that it will marginalize GoPro products could destroy GoPro's appeal more than Apple already has.

Consequently, GoPro's stock tanked. It went from $40 to $10 in just one year. And a few years after that, it went to about $5, and the investor's entire investment was essentially wiped out.

The investor made that costly mistake all because he misjudged his circle of competence. He thought GoPro was in his circle of competence because he used and liked its products. In particular, he thought he knew whether consumers would like GoPro's products because he used them. In reality, he didn't. He was completely wrong about the product's prospects.

At the end of the day, he didn't know what mattered to the consumer. Consider this. You know many of the 80/20 reasons why you like shopping on Amazon over other retail locations, such as:

- Fast, 2-day shipping
- Easier to buy with a click
- Decent prices
- Don't need to visit many stores
- Comparing many products is easy

Knowing those reasons allows you to assess Amazon's competitive strength. It allows you to ask yourself, "what are the chances of Walmart offering faster shipping than Amazon? What are the chances a competitor could offer lower prices? What are the chances a competitor could steal customers by developing a better website experience?" In the end, answering those questions allows you to get a sense of the risks involved with Amazon.

But for cameras, most investors wouldn't be able to do that very easily. Unlike how most people have a decent sense of why they shop at Amazon over retail locations, they don't have that same understanding with cameras.

Obviously, most people know that price and camera quality are important. However, there are many other factors that matter to the consumer—factors that some consumers aren't even aware of.

Consider convenience. Consumers like products that are more accessible. That meant that over time, GoPro would have had difficulty competing against the iPhone because using a camera that's attached to a phone is far easier than carrying a separate camera (assuming that GoPro couldn't makes its camera quality exponentially better than that of the iPhone).

But many consumers aren't aware of the fact that convenience is an important factor. It's simply a very subtle factor. When consumers buy cameras, they very consciously look at the price and camera quality, so they know that those factors are important. But the consideration of convenience happens more subconsciously since consumers don't think about it as much. As a result, an investor who owns cameras may not even know that convenience is an important determinant of buying behavior.

In fact, that happened to the GoPro investor. He didn't think about the convenience factor, even though he owned two GoPros. He simply thought that GoPro's product would be competitive over the long term due to its growing brand strength and high camera quality. After all, those were the factors that he spent the most time thinking about when buying his two GoPros. As a result, he ended up overlooking an important determinant of GoPro's long-term ability to attract consumers.

That illustrates an important point. You can own a product and love it. But, at the same time, you may not truly understand the business itself and why consumers like its products.

Coca-Cola is one these companies. Coca-Cola is a very simple business, and every investor has tried its products. Consequently, many investors think they understand the consumer behavior behind Coca-Cola's success. In reality, many of them don't.

If you ask an individual why they drink Coca-Cola or Pepsi, they are going to say, "because it tastes better" or "because I'm loyal to this brand." Those are the most logical things to say. In reality, however, we discovered that the average consumer can't easily differentiate between the two colas, nor are they loyal to any particular brand.

Even if a consumer identified that branding had something to do with Coca-Cola's success, they would have still overlooked another important factor: distribution strength.

Consider this.

Pepsi is not an option in many places where people want colas.

If you go to McDonald's, you cannot get a Pepsi. They only sell Coca-Cola.

If you go to Subway, you cannot get a Pepsi. They only sell Coca-Cola.

If you go to Burger King, you cannot get a Pepsi. They only sell Coca-Cola.

Coca-Cola prevents many prominent restaurants from distributing Pepsi. They do so by making them sign exclusive distribution agreements which specifically state that if they sell Coca-Cola, they can't sell certain competing products like Pepsi.

That obviously gives Coca-Cola a huge advantage. Consumers will always buy products that are easier to buy. That's why Coca-Cola and Pepsi started using vending machines in the first place. It's a lot easier to buy a cola if there is a vending machine in your school or workplace than if you had to go all the way to the store. Similarly, it is much easier to buy Coca-Cola over Pepsi if the restaurant that you are at doesn't sell Pepsi. If Coca-Cola is available and Pepsi isn't, it's simply highly improbable that you would leave the restaurant to merely get a Pepsi.

Despite the importance of Coca-Cola's distribution capabilities in driving consumer behavior, most consumers don't know about it. In fact, if you had asked me why I drink Coca-Cola a few years ago, I wouldn't have mentioned its distribution capabilities. At the time, I had never looked deeply at Coca-Cola, so I wouldn't have known that its distribution strategy played a big role in driving consumer behavior. Therefore, I would have overlooked one of the most important determinants of why people drink Coca-Cola over Pepsi.

Therefore, you, an investor, could be a very avid Coca-Cola drinker. You could love the product. But you may still not understand why you are buying Coca-Cola in the first place.

Steve Jobs once said that he "never [relies] on market research" because consumers don't know what they want. They don't always know why they buy product A or product B. That's something that you need to remember. You can be a drinker of Coca-Cola. But you don't necessarily know why you are drinking it. You might be a fan of GoPro, but that doesn't mean you know what matters to the consumer.

As Warren Buffett once said:

> The first thing I have to decide when somebody calls me is within my circle of competence. I don't know how to value Microsoft. I don't know how to value Oracle.... And when I say understand, I don't mean understand how to use a computer or not use a computer in terms of a computer company.

"CONSISTENT CASH FLOWS, PREDICTABLE BUSINESS"

· ·

Another common way that investors decide whether a company is within their circle of competence is its revenue and free cash flow consistency.[2] In particular, investors often believe that companies

---

2   Free cash flow is a measure of a company's profitability. It represents how much cash the company produced in profit.

that have a history of producing consistent levels of revenues and profits are understandable. For example, I've seen people say things along the lines of, "This company has a long history of growing its revenue over time at roughly 5% per year. Therefore, I think that I can have a high degree of confidence that it will continue to grow at a roughly similar rate in the future."

On the surface, it can sound logical to conclude that companies that produce consistent free cash flows are within your circle of competence. Why wouldn't they be? If a company has been growing its revenue by 5% per year for the last decade, would it not be logical to say that it has a high chance of growing by 5% next year?

However, what some investors don't realize is that this sort of thinking is flawed because it is not driver-focused. To understand what I mean by "driver- focused," let's consider a hypothetical example.

Let's say that you are a phenomenal software engineer who has worked at some of the world's leading big tech companies: Meta, Netflix, Apple, and Google. However, you are considering leaving your current job at Google and working at another big tech company, Amazon, in order to try something new. But you're not ready to apply yet. You first want to assess your chances of actually landing the job. Going through an interview process can be extremely time- consuming, and you don't have much free time to spare as a busy software developer.

There are two ways you could assess your chances of landing the job: by using history or by analyzing drivers.

Using history would involve looking at your past ability to land a job in order to judge whether you are likely to land the job at Amazon. In your case, you would conclude that you would have a high chance of landing a job at Amazon. You've previously landed jobs at several other companies that are as competitive as Amazon—companies like Meta, Netflix, and Apple. Therefore, there is a good chance that you'll be a strong candidate at Amazon.

Analyzing drivers, on the other hand, involves breaking down the outcome into its drivers. In this case, it would mean breaking down the chance of landing the job (the outcome) into the factors that determine your chances of landing a job—factors such as resume quality, cultural fit, and the competition (the drivers). You would analyze such drivers to estimate the probabilities of landing the role, the outcome.

Both approaches have their advantages and disadvantages. The advantage of using the history approach is that it is quick and easy. It only takes a couple of seconds to realize that you have a sound history of landing competitive jobs, allowing you to reasonably conclude that you'll likely land a similarly competitive job at Amazon.

The main disadvantage with the history approach is that it is much more likely to lead to inaccurate conclusions.

With the history approach, you are assuming that the past is just like the present. You're assuming that Amazon's applicant pool is not more competitive than Google's applicant pool. You're assuming that your Amazon resume is just as good as your Google resume. You assuming that you'll fit into Amazon's culture just as well as you fit into Google's culture. If those assumptions don't hold true, you wouldn't be a competitive applicant at Amazon. In that case, the fact that you got into Google wouldn't be a good predictor of getting into Amazon.

On the other hand, the driver approach will yield far more accurate conclusions. With the driver approach, you are examining the major factors that influence your chances of landing the job. You're not assuming that Amazon's applicant pool is just as competitive as Google's. You're actually analyzing it in order to determine how competitive the applicants are. You're not assuming that you're a good cultural fit at Amazon because you were a good cultural fit at Google. You're actually assessing Amazon's culture to see if you would be a good fit. Therefore, the driver approach would allow you to better predict whether you would land the job.

In the stock market, many investors use the history method to determine whether they understand a business and whether they can predict it. As mentioned earlier, they make statements along the lines of, "this company's sales have been consistently growing at 5% over the past 10 years, so I can be reasonably confident that the company will grow at a similar rate over the next several years."

Using the history method in the hypothetical job example wouldn't have caused any issues. Google and Amazon recruit similar kinds of individuals, so the competitiveness of applicants at each firm is fairly similar. However, in the stock market, the history method usually leads to poor outcomes.

Remember, the history method assumes that the past is like the present. It assumes that the factors that drive sales—brand strength, consumer tastes, and management quality—are the same in the past and the present. However, that rarely holds true in the world of business. Brand strengths, the competitive environment, and management qualities change over time. As a result, the past doesn't have to be a good indicator of the future.

In fact, businesses that have had long histories of growing can see reversals as things change.

Consider the case of ConocoPhillips. In late 2007 and early 2008, Warren Buffett purchased over $7 billion of stock in ConocoPhillips, an oil and natural gas company. ConocoPhillips had a long and strong history of seeing sales grow. From 2000-2008, it had grown sales by more than 500%. To many investors, that would have indicated that it would be a sound investment. At the very least, many investors were thinking that sales would continue to roar. That's what the trend was, after all.

But everyone—including Warren Buffett—was wrong.

Oil and gas prices tanked right after Buffett invested in ConocoPhillips. Consequently, historical sales trends reversed, and sales fell by well over 50%. And in 2009, Warren Buffett ended up selling over half of his ConocoPhillips stake at a loss.

Buffett recounts in Berkshire Hathaway's 2008 annual report that he didn't think ConocoPhillips's sales would fall:

Without urging from Charlie or anyone else, I bought a large amount of ConocoPhillips stock when oil and gas prices were near their peak. I in no way anticipated the dramatic fall in energy prices that occurred in the last half of the year. I still believe the odds are good that oil sells far higher in the future than the current $40-$50 price. But so far, I have been dead wrong. Even if prices should rise, moreover, the terrible timing of my purchase has cost Berkshire several billion dollars.

ConocoPhillips looked steady, but its sales unexpectedly plummeted

Conoco Phillips Revenue ($ in millions) from 2000 to 2022

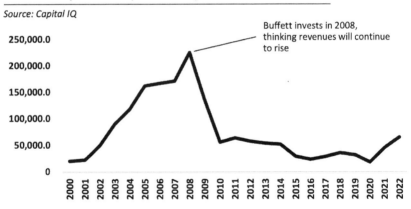

Source: Capital IQ

Or take McDonald's—a business that dominates a slow-ly-changing industry—as an example. From 1990 to 2012, McDon-ald's has grown its revenues almost every single year. It even grew its revenues from 2007-2010—through the great financial crisis. In 2010, some investors would have said, "McDonald's will surely grow over the next 5 or 10 years. It has a consistent track record of grow-ing over the past several decades, so I'm confident that it won't, at the very least, decline in the future." But that's exactly what ended up happening. From 2014-2018, McDonald's sales declined by 25%. McDonald's—a business that many view as being nearly invincible—lost a quarter of its sales in just a few years.

MCD's sales looked steady, but historical trends reversed

McDonald's revenue ($ in millions) from 1990-2022

Source: Capital IQ

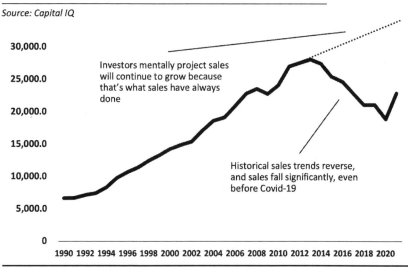

The driver method could have revealed that the past wasn't like the present. An investor analyzing drivers would have analyzed the determinants of McDonald's sales. In the process, they would have realized that one of those determinants—consumer needs and wants—were changing. Consumers have become more health conscious, reducing the chances that they would choose McDonald's. As a result, an investor focused on drivers would have realized that the past wasn't like the future.

Moreover, one of the big dangers of using the history method is that it can cause you to lose confidence in your stocks during turbulent times.

One time, I was analyzing a major technology company that's worth billions of dollars, and it was also—by far—one of the most dominant companies in its niche. At the time, the company had been growing sales at phenomenally high rates. For about 5 years, it consistently grew sales at 30%-50% per year. So, I said to myself, "this company must continue to grow at high rates in the future. It will grow sales by 15% at the very least."

I was dead wrong.

Just a few weeks after buying the stock, growth unexpectedly slowed down—a lot. The company reported year over year sales growth of only 10%, which was much lower than their 30%-50% track record. The slowdown surprised Wall Street as well, causing the stock price to fall by 40%+.

At that moment, I had lost a large degree of confidence in the security. I didn't sell, but I was far less confident in the business. Since I used the history method, I didn't have any evidence to prove that the growth slowdown was only temporary. The company's financial history was my only tool to predict the future, and that financial history was only getting worse. Therefore, the best (and only) conclusion I could draw was that the company was going to get worse.

The outcome would have been different had I used the driver method.

For one, I would have been far more likely to realize that such a high growth rate was unsustainable. One driver of a company's growth is the market size. If a company is pursuing a large market, there is a large potential to grow. But this wasn't the case—at all. In hindsight, I realized that they had previously grown so fast that they had penetrated nearly the entire market, making a sudden slowdown inevitable.

The driver method would have also allowed me to be more confident in my stock. Since I didn't take the driver approach, I didn't have evidence to support how fast I thought the company would grow except that "it had grown at a stable rate over the previous few years." The fact that I didn't have evidence became problematic when Wall Street turned bearish. At that point in time, I couldn't point to any evidence that would prove that Wall Street was wrong about the company's long-term growth, making it difficult to be greedy when others were fearful.

It's important, then, to realize that you never understand a business merely because it has produced a consistent stream of sales and profits. Remember Coca-Cola? Over many decades, Coca-Cola has consistently grown its sales. But does that mean investors understand it? No, many investors don't really understand it. Or consider Apple. From 2010-2020, Apple has grown sales in every quarter except for 5 of them. But does that mean Charlie Munger understands Apple? Of course not. As he has said, he is not an "expert" on Apple.

This section, then, begs an important question: how do you really know whether you understand a business? "If a company's revenue and cash flow consistency doesn't determine whether I understand a business, what does? How can I know whether I understand a business?"

All your questions will be answered in the next section. I'll explain a concept called "The Second Layer of Competence" that will help you understand how Outlier Investors determine whether they understand a business.

Outlier Investors never assume simple businesses are understandable.

The Second Layer of Competence

In the early 2000s, many investors classified Amazon as being a speculative company.

Amazon wasn't a simple business. The internet was still fairly new, and not all investors grasped what online shopping meant.

Amazon didn't produce consistent profits. If anything, it had a track record of seeing its net losses grow.

Amazon wasn't in a slowly changing industry. It was a technology company, where new companies were being born every day.

Consequently, most investors would have said that they couldn't predict Amazon's future. "Unlike the cola niche, the technology space changes every few years. No profit track record means I don't know whether the company will be successful. Amazon hasn't convinced me to stop shopping at Walmart, so I don't know whether it will convince other people as well."

But there was one Outlier: Nick Sleep.

Nick Sleep, the co-founder of the Nomad Investment Partnership, had a different view of Amazon. While most investors classified Amazon as being an unpredictable business, Nick Sleep didn't. In the early 2000s, Nick Sleep felt comfortable predicting that Amazon would be a successful business over the long term.

Nick noticed that Amazon benefited from a concept known as shared economies of scale. It said that Amazon's competitive advantage and sales would grow like a self-fulfilling cycle. Think about it. As Amazon gets more sales, they get more profit. More profit means that they can reinvest more money into improving the customer experience and reducing costs, allowing them to offer lower prices. Lower prices and a better customer experience means more customers would be attracted to Amazon. More customers mean more profit. More profit means Amazon can reinvest into improving the customer experience and into lowering prices. A better customer experience and lower prices means they attract more customers. And the cycle repeats.[3]

Nick Sleep noticed that Amazon's growth was a self-fulfilling cycle

A recreation of Jeff Bezos' "napkin sketch"

Source: Steady Compounding

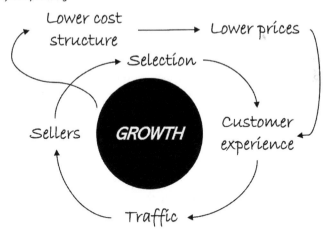

Over time, Nick Sleep realized that this would allow Amazon to build a strong advantage over its competitors. In particular, he noticed that Amazon would always be able to charge a lower price

---

3   This explanation is slightly simplified so that it is easy for new investors to understand.

than competitors, allowing it to become the dominant e-commerce player.

So, Nick Sleep made a huge bet on it. He concentrated his entire investment fund's capital in three stocks: Berkshire Hathaway, Costco, and, of course, Amazon.

And it did phenomenally well. Over the 13 years his investment fund was open, he delivered 921.1% returns, compared to 116.9% of the MSCI World Index. Amazon, in particular, had grown so much that it represented over 70% of his net worth at one point.

What's interesting was that Nick Sleep was able to predict Amazon's future accurately and bring it within his circle of competence far before anyone else—even though it didn't fit the prototype of what people call an understandable business.

People often say, "I understand Coca-Cola because it has a simple business model." But, as we mentioned earlier, most people don't understand Coca-Cola, even though it is a simple business. Moreover, Nick Sleep understood Amazon, even though it was a fairly complicated business at the time.

People often say, "I understand ConocoPhillips's future because it has a long, consistent trend of growing sales." But, as we previously saw, the fact that a company has a long history of producing profits doesn't mean that you know where it is heading in the future. On top of that, Nick Sleep was able to predict Amazon's future, even though it didn't have a good profit track record at all.

People often say, "I understand GoPro because I use and like the product." But, as we recently saw, an investor can like and use a product, but they can also be totally wrong about whether it will succeed. In fact, Nick Sleep's "shared economies of scale" insight couldn't have been picked up by merely being a consumer of Amazon.

So, how did Nick Sleep bring Amazon within his circle of competence?

In my view, he developed what I call a Second Layer of Competence. The concept is fairly straightforward.

The difference between the first and second layer of competence

Name	Definition	Importance
First layer of competence	<ul><li>Represents factors that drive a company's competitive advantage</li><li>For Coca-Cola, examples include brand strength and product quality</li></ul>	<ul><li>Tells you about the competitive *positioning* of a business</li><li>Informs you how successful a business is today</li></ul>
Second layer of competence	<ul><li>Represents factors that drive the first layer of competence</li><li>For a brand, examples include the size of marketing budget and the CMO's quality</li></ul>	<ul><li>Tells you about the competitive *velocity* of a business</li><li>Allows you to predict how successful businesses will be in the future</li></ul>

As the name suggests, there are two layers to your circle of competence.

The first layer is a set of high-level factors that drive a company's competitive advantage. Factors in the first layer are easy to identify. Some common ones include product quality, brand strength, culture, management quality, and cost efficiency.

The second layer is a list of drivers for the first-layer factors. It is a list of characteristics that can increase or decrease a company's positioning in each of those first-layer factors. For McDonald's, brand strength would be an important, easy-to-identify, first-layer factor. The second layer would then include a list of drivers that can increase or decrease McDonald's brand strength: the style of advertising, brand associations, the CMO's quality, the marketing mix, etc.

Unlike the first-layer factors, second-layer drivers are not easy to identify. In all likelihood, you cannot know what these drivers are without doing research. You can know that it is important for a restaurant to have a strong brand (a first- layer factor) without doing research, but you cannot know what actually makes a brand stronger or weaker (second-layer drivers) unless you do research. Moreover, second-layer drivers are more likely to be specific to a particular company or industry. For example, a strong culture, a first-layer factor, is important to virtually every company. However, the second-layer drivers that determine whether a firm has the right culture will differ from firm to firm. A company that's competing against Tesla would need a culture that fosters innovation, whereas a low-cost shoe manufacturer would need a culture that fosters frugality. Similarly, product quality is an important, first-layer factor in every company. But the second-layer drivers that determine whether a product is high-quality vary from industry to industry. In the beverage niche, product quality is important, and that is determined by the taste of the drink. In the book publishing niche, product quality is also important, but how the book tastes doesn't matter. Instead, insightfulness is what counts.

A partial illustration of the second layer of competence of McDonald's

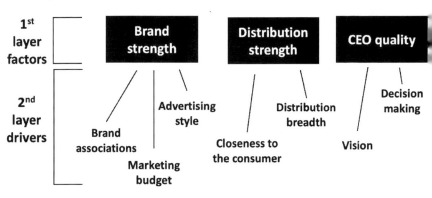

When many investors evaluate businesses, they usually only evaluate the first layer, not the second layer. They recognize that

Coca-Cola has a strong brand. But they don't understand what can make Coca-Cola's brand stronger or weaker. Is how many people know the brand key? How they perceive it? What role does the packaging play? What sorts of marketing campaigns can make the brand stronger?

They notice that Apple has a great product. But they don't know what about Apple's products make them so attractive. Is it the design? The features? The price? Or something else?

They can determine that customers like GoPro's product. But they don't understand what levers a company can pull to increase or decrease their product's appeal to customers.

If you can build a second layer of competence when evaluating a business, there is a good chance that you'll know where it is heading.

In a physics sense, first-layer factors tell you about the current position of an object. They tell you about the current competitive positioning of a business. Knowing that McDonald's has a strong brand and a great product tells you that McDonald's is a competitive business today.

Second-layer drivers are, in a sense, like the velocity of an object. They help you understand where a business is heading. Knowing that McDonald's has a strong brand today doesn't mean that it will have a strong brand tomorrow. But knowing that they are running intelligent brand marketing campaigns can inform you that they will have a strong brand tomorrow. Knowing that they have a phenomenal CMO can inform you that they will have a stronger brand in the future and knowing that they recently hired a dumb CMO can inform you that they will have a weaker brand in the future.

In fact, you'll notice that many of the best investors go to second-layer drivers when analyzing businesses.

Take Nick Sleep as an example. Many people analyzing Amazon in 2003 would have focused on first-layer drivers and said, "Amazon is not a competitive business. It doesn't have a low-cost advantage, the ability to sustainably offer customers lower prices. It doesn't have a track record of producing profits. It doesn't have a strong brand today. It doesn't have a base of loyal customers. Therefore, the business is weak and speculative."

But Nick Sleep thought differently. He didn't say, "Amazon is a weak company because it doesn't offer customers competitive prices today." Instead, he sought to understand the second-layer drivers that can increase or decrease a company's ability to offer products at competitive prices. That's what his shared economies of scale idea was all about.

Similarly, Nick Sleep knew that Amazon would develop a loyal customer base over time. Unlike some investors who only looked at first-layer factors and said, "Amazon is weaker than Walmart because Amazon doesn't have a large, loyal customer base," Nick focused on second-layer drivers. He asked himself about the drivers that could increase or decrease the size of Amazon's loyal customer base. Then he concluded that customers would start to develop loyalty towards Amazon since it would likely offer a better customer experience, lower prices, and fast shipping. So, he decided that Amazon would have a large loyal customer base in the future.

Or consider Warren Buffett. During a 1997 Berkshire Hathaway annual meeting, Buffett was asked a question about consumer behavior. When answering it, Buffett predicted that Coca-Cola would continue to prosper in the future by going to second-layer drivers:

> Now, virtually every person in the globe—maybe, well, let's get it down to 75% of the people in the globe—have some notion in their mind[s] about Coca-Cola... A year from now, it will be established in more minds, and it will have a slightly, slightly, slightly, different, overall position.

Buffett didn't say that Coca-Cola would continue to grow because it has a long track record of growing. That may have made him confident that it would continue to grow. But it wasn't the reason why he said it would continue to grow.

Buffett didn't say that Coca-Cola would continue to grow because it has a strong brand, a first-layer factor. Of course, that may have made him confident that it would continue to grow. But the fact that Coca-Cola has a strong brand today wasn't the reason why he said it would continue to grow.

Instead, Buffett went to the second-layer drivers of brand strength that can increase or decrease a brand's competitive positioning: how many people have Coca-Cola strongly "established" in their minds. At the end of the day, brands like Coca-Cola grow if the brand is more strongly established in the minds of more consumers. The more people know the brand, the more people can potentially buy it. And the stronger the brand is established, the more likely that they will end up buying it. Therefore, to get a grasp on a brand's future, the most important things to get a handle on would be those two second-layer drivers: how many people know the brand and how strongly it is established in the minds of every individual.

Therefore, the key to understanding a business is to be able to get to second-layer drivers.

You don't want to be the investor who says, "I understand Coca-Cola because it has a strong brand and because it produces consistent cash flows. Therefore, I believe that it will be competitive in the future." That's not a sound train of logic. In that case, you're simply arguing that Coca-Cola will be competitive in the future because it has a strong brand today. Of course, that's not a logical statement. A brand is never competitive in the future because it is competitive today. A brand is only competitive in the future because it is competitive in the future.

Instead, you want to be the investor who says, "I understand Coca-Cola because I understand its second-layer drivers. Coca-Cola brand's strength (a first-layer factor) is important to its success. But the fact that Coca-Cola has a strong brand today doesn't mean that Coca-Cola will be competitive in the future. To truly understand whether Coca-Cola will be competitive in the future, I must understand Coca-Cola's second-layer drivers—the drivers that could either increase or decrease Coca-Cola's brand strength, product quality, and distribution strength."

Two factors determine whether a business is within your circle of competence.

The first is whether you can merely identify the second-layer drivers of a business. If you can't identify the second-layer drivers of a business, you simply don't understand it. This is the reason why people don't understand Coca-Cola. They definitely have a first layer of competence around Coca-Cola.

They know that Coca-Cola has a great product.

They know that Coca-Cola has a strong brand.

And, hopefully, at least a few investors know that Coca-Cola is one of the best distributed consumer products in history.

But most investors can't identify Coca-Cola's second-layer drivers. In other words, they haven't built a second layer of competence around Coca-Cola. They don't know what can make Coca-Cola's brand stronger or weaker. They don't understand how being closely associated with happiness is vital to Coca-Cola's competitive positioning. They don't know how easy or hard it would be for Pepsi to take market share if they simply decided to spend more money on marketing. As a result, they can't evaluate whether Coca-Cola will be stronger or weaker in the future other than by merely guessing.

However, it is not enough to be able to identify the second-layer drivers of a business. You also must be able to predict how those drivers will play out over the long term. This second reason likely explains why Charlie Munger said Apple wasn't within his circle of competence.

In all likelihood, he understood the second-layer drivers of Apple's strength. He likely knew what could cause Apple's brand to rise and fall. As someone who has deeply studied brands like Coca-Cola, Munger likely knew what could cause Apple's brand to fail or succeed in the future. Similarly, he likely understood the second-layer drivers of its product quality. As someone who has studied the successes and failures of consumer products over the past decade, he had at least a basic understanding of what causes products to fail or succeed. "So why doesn't Munger understand Apple? After all, he likely knows some of the important second-layer drivers that could make it succeed or fail."

The answer is simple. Munger didn't feel as if he could predict how those second-layer drivers would impact Apple in the future. Munger has frequently said that he doesn't understand technology companies. There is a good reason why. It's hard to predict how the second-layer drivers of a business will play out in the future. Take Apple as an example. It's easy to understand that product quality is an important, first-layer factor. And, with some research, it's not too difficult to understand that a phone's user interface is an important second-layer driver of product quality. However, what is hard to evaluate is whether Apple will have a more or less competitive user interface in the future. In the tech industry, things can change rapidly. Innovative tech companies can improve the quality of their products very quickly. As a result, it's hard for investors like Munger to know whether Apple or Android will have a better designed phone and user interface 5 or 10 years from now. It's not difficult to understand that user interface quality is an important second-layer driver of product quality. But it's not easy for Munger to understand whether Apple will have the best interface in the future.

Therefore, two things need to hold true for a business to be within your circle of competence. First, you must be able to identify the second-layer drivers of a business. If you can identify that Coca-Cola has a strong brand today, that's great. But you shouldn't feel as if you can predict its future unless you understand the second-layer drivers that could increase or decrease its brand strength and product quality over the long-term. Second, you must be able to understand how those drivers will play out in the future. If you can understand that the iPhone's design and user interface are important determinants of its product quality, that's great. But you shouldn't feel as if you understand Apple's future unless you can be sure that Apple will have a superior design and interface over the long term.

Whenever you're evaluating a company, you should list the first-layer factors that are important in the business. For new investors, it can even be helpful to rank those factors from most important to least important. That will help you prioritize your research. More importantly, it will get your mind jogging about which factors really matter in a business and which ones don't.

Then, write down a list of second-layer drivers that determine a company's positioning in first-layer factors. If product quality is important in an industry, write down what makes a good or bad product. If branding is important, write down what makes a brand stronger or weaker.

Finally, assess the business on both the first-layer factors and second-layer drivers. Understanding how a business stands on first-layer factors will give you a sense of how competitive a business is today. That, of course, is helpful for making investment decisions. But to really understand whether a company will be stronger or weaker in the future—and the degree to which it will be stronger or weaker—you must go to second-layer drivers.

Don't just understand the competitive position of a business. Understand its competitive velocity, too. As Buffett once said, "I skate to where the puck is going to be, not to where it has been."

Average investors research a company's competitive positioning.

Outlier Investors research what drives its competitive positioning.

Follow The 80%
Past Rule

One evening, Charlie Munger and Mohnish Pabrai were having dinner together. In the middle of the dinner, Munger casually told Pabrai that he wanted to learn about General Motors' history.

In response, Pabrai simply suggested getting that information from a stock-research website: "You can see long histories of the business in something like Value Line."

"No, that's not what I'm talking about. I want a hundred-year history of GM, and I want a hundred years of numbers for GM," Munger replied.

Pabrai didn't know where one could get such old annual reports, and the conversation about General Motors died down for the night.

Many weeks later, Pabrai was giving a talk at Boston University. As part of his presentation, he was doing an analysis of American Express for the students. To help contribute to his analysis, one of the students casually mentioned that Boston University had American Express annual reports going all the way back to the 1950s.

Pabrai then recognized that the school kept many old annual reports, and he remembered that Munger was looking for some old annual reports as well. Putting two and two together, he asked the students if they had old annual reports on General Motors. The students said that they did. In fact, they had over 24,000 pages of annual reports going all the way back to 1912, which Pabrai then gave to Munger.

You might be wondering, "It's great that Munger was able to get 100 years' worth of General Motors annual reports, but why did he even want them in the first place? Why does it matter if he knows how much money General Motors was making back in 1912?"

Well, Pabrai once told the story that I just told you to a different group of university students, and he recognized that they would have the same question: "Why did Munger even want such old annual reports in the first place?" So, Pabrai provided the students with a simple explanation: Munger wanted to "just [get] better at knowing how the world works."

Munger's behavior is a perfect example of the 80% Past Rule. Spend 80% of your time researching history to learn why businesses succeed and fail, and 20% of your time studying the present to make investment decisions.

Most people research a stock by learning about its present situation. For example, they read about current industry trends to predict the future of a company. They read current annual reports to get a company's recent financial data. They assess the company's current management team. They read current news articles to learn about what's going on in the world. And they compile their up-to-date research to make a buying or selling decision.

Successful investors, on the other hand, take a different approach. They don't focus most of their research efforts on understanding the present situation of a company. Instead, they study the past. Take Warren Buffett's research on Coca-Cola as an example.

Coca-Cola was a highly attractive investment when Buffett bought the stock in 1988. For one thing, it was a high-quality company that had a strong brand. Moreover, the high-quality company would have been regarded as quite cheap by many investors since Buffett had bought Coca-Cola just a few months after Black Monday, the 1987 stock market crash. Being "greedy when others [were] fearful" meant the 1987 crash created the perfect buying opportunity.

The attractiveness of Coca-Cola's business makes many people think that it was a quick investment decision to make. After all, how much research did Buffett actually need to do? The business was strong, and it was cheap. What else did he need to know?

Well, it turns out that the investment decision wasn't very quick.

Buffett not only had to read Coca-Cola's and Pepsi's recent annual reports to make the investment decision, but also, he had to do a deep analysis of Coca-Cola's history by reading over a decade's worth of annual reports. That's right. He read more than 10 years' worth of Coca-Cola annual reports before making the investment decision. In other words, he read more outdated annual reports than up-to-date annual reports.

Or consider Buffett's investment in Bank of America. CNBC's Becky Quick once asked Buffett how he conducted research for his Bank of America investment. How did Buffett respond? He did not say that he merely read Bank of America's most recent annual report. He didn't merely say that he read Bank of America's last 10 annual reports. Nor did he say that he read its last 25 annual reports. Instead, he responded by saying that he read every single Bank of America annual report over the past 50 years before making the investment.

The reason he focused on reading outdated annual reports is very simple.

Your brain is a predictive machine. It is always using its knowledge to predict the outcome of events. When you submit a resume, your brain is assessing the chances that you'll land a job. When you buy a product, your brain attempts to assess whether you'll get bang for your buck. The same is true in the stock market. Your brain is always trying to predict the chances that a business will succeed or fail.

Your brain is always relying on historical data to make those predictions. When you need to make a prediction, your brain retrieves information that could help make an accurate prediction. Let's say that you are analyzing Coca-Cola's stock. When doing so, your brain will automatically retrieve any information on

Coca-Cola that can help you predict its future. It will retrieve your knowledge about how often consumers choose Coca-Cola over Pepsi, how often large brands fail, and similar kinds of information.

However, our predictive machines aren't always perfect at predicting the future. Most people have submitted a resume, thinking that they would land the job for sure, but ended up not even landing the first-round interview. Most people have purchased products that ended up being a total waste of money, and every investor has miscalculated the risk and reward of a security.

Assuming people are rational, the main reason people make poor predictions is that they don't have the right data in their minds.

Sometimes people don't have enough data. Not having enough data caused one individual I know to miss out on nearly doubling his net worth with minimal risk. Most people know that it is generally better to invest in index funds over mutual funds. Index funds have lower fees and earn comparable returns. But I knew an individual who had never heard of index funds. He just put everything in his actively managed mutual funds and forgot about it. So, he ended up paying high fees for most of his life (and ended up underperforming the market as well). After doing the math, we learned that his investment portfolio could have been worth about 75% more had he heard of index funds and known about their benefits—with minimal incremental risk. Therefore, simply not having enough data on investment options cost him the potential to almost double his investment portfolio.

Other times, people don't have correct data. I remember one time I was applying for an internship in college. The role didn't seem that competitive. LinkedIn said that there were no more than a few dozen applicants. Therefore, I thought it would be easy to land the role. A couple of months went by, and I ended up landing an interview at the company. I told my professor, Mr. Murphy, the good news since he was always interested in our career accomplishments. Moreover, I told him that I thought that I had a good shot at getting in because the role didn't seem very competitive. In response, however, I got some unexpected news. He told me that the role was actually extremely competitive. I was confused. "How could it be competitive if there weren't even many applicants?" It turns out that I didn't have the correct data. The "applicant count" on LinkedIn wasn't a good proxy of the applicant pool's competitiveness because I realized that they got a lot of their applications through other postings as well. In the end, I got rejected. I predicted that I would easily land the role, but I was wrong because I didn't have the right data.

Therefore, your mind is only as good as the data it has. If it is oblivious to important pieces of data, it will make a bad prediction (that's what happened to the guy who hadn't heard of index funds). If it is running on incorrect information, it will make incorrect conclusions (that's why I miscalculated the chances of landing the internship).

To make investment decisions in particular, you need data on why businesses succeed. Successful investing is about predicting 1) which businesses will succeed or fail and 2) the degree to which they will succeed or fail. Your ability to make those predictions is dependent upon the data you have. If your mind has lots of accurate data on why businesses succeed or fail, it will be able to make good predictions (assuming you stay rational). If it doesn't, you can only make an educated guess.

That's where reading old annual reports comes in. Old annual reports are just pools of information on why businesses succeed and fail. They contain large amounts of information on the decisions management teams have made and how those decisions impacted the business. Therefore, if you start to read old annual reports, you'll start to absorb a lot of information on why businesses succeed and fail. Hence, your mind will have better data to predict which businesses will succeed and fail in the future.

In fact, some of the biggest investment failures have occurred because outdated data was overlooked. Take Ray Dalio as an example.

Back in 1982, Mexico defaulted on its debts. The default spread fear in the financial markets. Of course, people are scared when any country defaults. But this wasn't a normal situation. It was scarier because things were expected to get worse. At the time, major U.S. banks had lent large sums of money to other countries that had similar risk levels to Mexico's. This meant that there was a high probability that many other countries would default, which could trigger a major financial crisis. In Ray Dalio's words, "there was a 75 percent chance [that]...the economy would move into failure."

Recognizing the instability in the economy, Ray Dalio assumed the worst would come. He went on the TV show *Wall $treet Week with Louis Rukeyser* and "declared" that a depression was coming. He invested in T-bills, futures, and gold—assets that he believed would perform the best in a worst-case scenario.

The problem for Ray Dalio was that his predictions weren't right. A crisis never ensued. The markets never crashed. In fact, the stock market ended up booming "by a record amount." Long story short, the Fed was able to lower interest rates and stimulate the economy—without causing hyperinflation. Moreover, the Fed and IMF (International Monetary Fund) were able to work with the debtor nations so that they could safely pay back their loans.

Being wrong was one of Ray Dalio's biggest setbacks. As he recounts in his book *Principles,* it felt like a "blow to the head" that had "cost [him] just about everything [he] had built at Bridgewater," putting him "back to square one." In short, it wrecked his reputation.

Reflecting on the incident many years later, Ray Dalio stated that that entire investment mistake was preventable by simply studying history:

> I again saw the value of studying history. What had happened, after all, was "another one of those."
> I should have realized that debts denominated in one's own currency can be successfully restructured with the government's help, and that when central banks simultaneously provide stimulus (as they

did in March 1932, and the low point of the Great
Depression, and as they did again in 1982), inflation
and deflation can be balanced against each other.
As in 1971, I had failed to recognize the lessons of
history.

Note that Ray Dalio didn't say that he would have improved his
investment prediction by studying the present. He didn't say that
he needed to do a deeper dive into what was going on in the economy at the time. He didn't need to learn more about what the Fed
was doing or what inflation was doing. He simply needed to study
the past.

Up-to-date information could only tell Ray Dalio what was currently going on in the world, but out-of-date information could tell
him what would happen in the future.

Someone once asked Charlie Munger how he would teach a
college course on finance if he ever had the opportunity. How did
he respond to the question? He didn't say that he would teach the
students how to calculate profit margins from an income statement. He didn't say that he would teach them how to use Excel to
build financial models. He didn't even say that he would teach the
students how to read an annual report. Instead, he said he would
have 100 different case studies on why businesses have succeeded
and failed in the past. Why? Once again, you must be able to deeply
study history to make investment decisions. If you don't know why
businesses have succeeded and failed in the past, you won't know
why they will succeed and fail in the future.

However, an important question remains: how do you actually
use annual reports to learn from history? "An annual report literally
has hundreds of pages. How do I know which pages to read? What
exactly am I looking for in an annual report?"

Truthfully, it depends. The important parts of an annual report
to read will vary from company to company. You might be studying a company that failed due to taking on too much debt. In that
case, analyzing the company's balance sheet would give you a good

sense of what "too much leverage" looks like. If you are studying a retailer that became outdated in the eyes of consumers, studying the balance sheet probably wouldn't be too insightful. The balance sheet tells you about a company's debt levels, but it doesn't provide much insight into how consumer trends can cause it to become outdated. Instead, reading about management's discussion of consumer trends would be more useful.

But there are two questions you can ask yourself to help identify the most important parts of an old annual report to read.

The first question is, "What key performance indicators (KPIs) have materially changed in the business during the period?" Have sales changed significantly? Have costs of goods sold increased materially? Have capital expenditures increased significantly? Or has something else changed?

The second question is, "What part of the annual report can tell me why this KPI has changed?"

The first question helps you focus on the most important thing to learn about in the annual report. At the end of the day, there are dozens and dozens of financial metrics in any annual report. You cannot understand every single one of them. By focusing on KPIs—a company's most important financial metrics—you are focusing on the best measures of a company's competitive strength.

The second question helps you identify the right part of the annual report to read. Remember, you always have one goal when reading old annual reports: understanding what can cause the business to succeed or fail. Asking yourself the second question makes you think about which part of the annual report will allow you to understand why businesses succeed and fail, allowing you to cut through irrelevant information.

In fact, the approach I just described is similar to that which Charlie Munger takes. Whenever Munger reads an old annual report, he is first trying to understand what KPIs changed in the business. Then, he tries to use the annual report to understand why it changed in that manner. As he said during a Berkshire Hathaway annual meeting:

> If I were teaching in a business school, I would have value-line-type figures that took people through the entire history of General Motors. And I would try to relate the changes in the graph and in the data to what happened in the business.[4]

If you think about it, though, you can't read everything in history. Let's say that you are analyzing an industry that has 5 major players. Each of those companies will publish an annual report. If you want to study twenty years of history, you have to read 100 annual reports. Each annual report might take at least an hour to read, so that is 100 hours of work for that one industry. On top of that, you probably won't find a good investment opportunity in the first company you analyze. You would need a lot of luck for the first industry you analyze to contain the perfect investment opportunity. So, you may need to analyze at least 5 different industries. That's 500 hours (or 20.8 days) of work.

That's not exactly feasible for most people. So, let me help you narrow your research focus by giving you guidance on what types of annual reports to read.

REPORT #1:
ANNUAL REPORTS OF COMPANIES THAT NO LONGER PUBLISH REPORTS

Charlie Munger has a well-known principle called the Invert Principle. The Invert Principle says that it is easier to solve a problem if you invert it; if you want to learn how to do something, first, you must learn how *not* to do it.

For example, let's say that you want to learn how to start a

---

4   Value line is a tool for researching stocks. It is known for having graphs of a company's KPIs—revenues, profits, and operating income—that go back a long time.

successful restaurant. The first thing that many people would do is learn how to start a successful restaurant. They would study major successes like McDonald's and Starbucks and try to reverse engineer their successes.

However, the Invert Principle would say to do the opposite. Instead of learning how to start a successful restaurant, the Invert Principle would say that you must learn how to start an unsuccessful restaurant in order to learn how to start a successful one. In other words, you would have to study why the no-name restaurants are failing to learn how to start the next McDonald's.

On the surface, the Invert Principle can sound somewhat strange. If you want to learn to start the next McDonald's, why is it important to study no-name restaurants? What can they teach you about how to run a restaurant? They don't know how to run a restaurant themselves. Why not just study the major success stories like McDonald's and Starbucks?

The reason is actually fairly straightforward.

In many areas of life, you can do many things right, but you will still fail if you make a big mistake. Take starting a restaurant as an example. You can have the best food in town. But if you don't know how to market your restaurant, no one will know about it. Then, they will eat at your competitors. Or take resumes as an example. You can have the best job qualifications. But if you spell something incorrectly, they will remember you as "the applicant that doesn't know grammar."

The same applies to investing. There can be many tailwinds for a business. But it only takes one big headwind to make all the other tailwinds meaningless.

For example, there were many sound reasons to invest in Blockbuster during the early 2000s. They were the largest player in the niche. They had a product and brand that people loved. There were large opportunities to grow market share since they didn't control about 75% of the market. When Blockbuster CEO John Antioco joined the company, he uncovered many opportunities to reduce costs and increase market share. Sales growth was strong. Between 1999 and 2003, sales grew from $4.4 billion to $5.9 billion.

But, in the end, all those tailwinds didn't matter. Netflix simply created a better product than Blockbuster, and Blockbuster ended up declaring bankruptcy.

The Invert Principle makes you aware of the 'one thing that could go wrong and wreck your investment.' If you only study successful businesses like McDonald's and Starbucks, you are highly unlikely to come across the 'one thing that could go wrong and wreck your investment.' The reason highly successful businesses are successful is that they avoid making major mistakes. As a result, you will never learn about the things that can go wrong in a business if you only study businesses where things didn't go wrong. On the other hand, if you study unsuccessful businesses, you will start to become aware of the things that can go wrong in a business.

Moreover, applying the Invert Principle helps makes your investment theses more balanced. If you only study successful businesses, you'll end up mainly learning about the factors that make businesses succeed. However, only studying successes will mainly strengthen your ability to assess the upside potential in a business. If you don't study failures, you are effectively not studying the risks that can occur in a business. You'll then overlook important risks. In the end, studying successes and not studying failures will likely cause you to be overconfident in your investments, which is the opposite of what you want.

In fact, studying failures is a common practice among many successful investors. During a Coca-Cola annual meeting, Coca-Cola CEO Muhtar Kent was interviewing Warren Buffett about his business philosophy. One of the insights that he revealed is that studying failures is an important part of his investment process: "I like to study failure, actually...We want to see what has caused businesses to go bad."

What you should do, then, is study the businesses where things did go wrong. If you are investing in McDonald's, you don't only want to read McDonald's annual reports. You should also read the annual reports of the restaurant that no one has ever heard of. You should be reading the annual report of the restaurant that went bankrupt last year. If you are investing in Netflix, you don't only want to read Netflix's annual reports. You should also be reading Blockbuster's annual reports. Even though Blockbuster is out of business today, you still want to read its annual reports if you plan on investing in Netflix today. Blockbuster's outdated annual reports can provide insights into the fundamental drivers of why businesses like Netflix can fail.

In my opinion, reading the annual reports of failed companies is one of the most important things that you can do. Not doing so means that you may end up overlooking a risk that could wreck your investment portfolio.

But, what's interesting is that no one ever studies failures. When was the last time someone you know read an annual report of a company that completely failed—a company that's no longer trading on the stock market? I would bet that most people wouldn't be able to recall a single instance of themselves or an acquaintance reading an annual report of a company that went out of business. Therefore, some of the most important annual reports to read are those that are never read.

REPORT #2:
CEO LETTERS AND ANNUAL REPORTS OF COMPANIES IN THEIR EARLY HISTORY

Every CEO and investor relations team ideally wants their company to look good. A CEO's compensation is often tied to the stock price of their company. The higher the stock price, the more they get paid. Moreover, investor relations teams view their job as making a company as good as possible. As Warren Buffett once said, "a lot of companies... have investor relations people, and they are dying just to pump out what they think is good news all the time."

To get investors excited, companies will highlight their financial performance. The people on Wall Street are finance people who like to build financial models and analyze financial statements. So, seeing strong sales growth and margins is what excites most investors.

Typically, strong, established companies don't have a problem finding financial metrics to highlight. Since they have strong competitive advantages, it is not difficult for them to have impressive margin and growth figures. So, CEOs of those types of companies will make their company look good by highlighting the company's strong financial performance.

However, companies that are in their infancy have a problem finding as many financial metrics to highlight. The financials of early-stage companies often don't look very impressive. The company will typically be losing money. They might be using a lot of debt to finance growth. There definitely won't be any dividends, and important KPIs like profit margins might be highly volatile.

So, early-stage companies won't only focus on financial metrics to entice investors. Instead, the CEOs of early-stage companies excite investors by talking about two things.

First, they talk about their vision for the business. Investors like to hear that there is a grandiose vision for a business. Especially when a business contains a lot of risk, investors like to hear that there is significant upside potential.

Second, CEOs will, more importantly, talk about how they will achieve their vision. Intelligent investors don't simply invest in a company because there is a lot of upside. If that were true, they would simply invest in every new tech company. Instead, they like to understand the CEO's plan for achieving their vision. How will they make their product better? What will they do to lower costs? How will they market and position their product?

You can take advantage of the fact that early-stage companies have a tendency to talk a lot about qualitative factors like business strategy.

Remember, to understand a business, you are trying to understand the factors that make it successful. You aren't trying to memorize the company's financial figures like profit margins and sales growth rates. You are trying to get a handle on the business strategy decisions that drive success and failure.

So, if you are trying to understand a company, it would be advantageous to read its annual report (and the CEO's Letter to Shareholders) from its early stages. These reports often contain a lot of information of the success drivers of the business. After all, that is what a company has to share with shareholders when they are just starting out. Since they can't highlight impressive financials, they highlight the reasons why they believe the company will succeed. That's exactly what you need to know to understand a business, and that's what is typically highlighted in the communications of early-stage companies.

For example, let's say that you are attempting to understand Amazon today. What you could do is read the company's most recent CEO Letters. That's what most people will do. Of course, there is nothing wrong with that.

But the problem with doing that is that it doesn't talk a lot about the fundamental reasons why Amazon is successful to begin with. Jeff Bezos' 2019 Letter to Shareholders is more about Amazon's current initiatives, such as their Diversity, Equity, and Inclusion initiatives and ESG initiatives. Moreover, Andy Jassy, the new CEO of Amazon, mainly talks more about financial KPIs and recent social initiatives in his 2021 Letter to Shareholders. (Though I will say that the CEO does a superb job of providing insights into its culture and helping investors understand how that has made the company successful).

To really get at the fundamental reasons why Amazon is successful today, you need to go back to Amazon's 1997 Letter to Shareholders, Jeff Bezos' first letter to investors. That's where Bezos has to sell a vision and lay out the reasons why Amazon will be successful. It's the letter that gets you to the drivers for why Amazon is successful today—drivers such as:

- An "easy-to-browse" and "easy-to-search" plat-
form
- 1-Click Buying
- "Vastly more reviews"
- Much more selection
- Being open 24 hours per day
- Affordable prices

These insights help you build your second layer of competence around Amazon. Virtually every investor knows that an
important first-layer factor for Amazon is its customer experience. However, not many investors know what second-layer
drivers can increase or decrease the quality of Amazon's customer experience; hence, not many investors know what could
make Amazon more or less successful. Jeff Bezos' 1997 Letter
to Shareholders, however, directly shares the most important
second-layer drivers of Amazon's success: selection, navigability, reviews, etc. Then, it simply becomes the job of an investor
to understand how those second-layer drivers will play out in
the future, allowing you to assess the competitive positioning of
Amazon's business in the future.

However, one thing astute readers will notice is that many of
the insights in Jeff Bezos' 1997 letter can be found in Amazon's
recent annual reports. In fact, a large portion of the "business over-
view" section is devoted to talking about the importance of the
customer experience. So, that begs an important question: what's
the point of reading Jeff Bezos' old CEO letter if some of the same
information can be found in current annual reports?

Well, the main advantage of reading old CEO letters over
recent annual reports is that old CEO letters are 80/20 or efficient.

Generally speaking, annual reports attempt to be exhaustive.
They try to cover every possible factor that can impact a firm's
operation. For example, Amazon's 2021 annual report contains
about 10 pages of almost every big risk you could think of in terms
of Amazon's business, including:

- Inventory risks
- Payment-related risks
- Supplier relationship risks
- Economics risks

But the problem is that many of the items listed in the annual report aren't the most important 80/20 drivers of Amazon's success. For example, it's not too important to be aware of the macroeconomic risks associated with investing in Amazon. The long-term profitability of any global e-commerce site has never been diminished merely due to a slight slowdown in the economy and some increases in the inflation rate. Therefore, focusing on how economic factors impact Amazon wouldn't be the best use of time. Similarly, it's not too important to be aware of payment-related risks such as fraud. Virtually all companies are exposed to a certain level of fraud-related risks, and it's not like Amazon is drastically less exposed to fraud-related risks than other Fortune 50 companies. So, you wouldn't get much closer to deciding whether Amazon or Walmart is a better stock by analyzing its fraud-related risks.

CEO letters, on the other hand, are more likely to be 80/20. While annual reports are usually at least one hundred pages, CEO letters are usually not more than a few pages. As a result, CEOs tend to be concise within their letters, forcing them to focus on the company's most important drivers. That was the case with Jeff Bezos' 1997 Letter to Shareholders. It focused on the most important drivers of Amazon's long-term competitive positioning: selection, navigability, and affordability.

Lastly, it's important to note that it can sometimes be preferable to read old CEO letters over old annual reports because CEO letters can offer a unique perspective.

It's important to keep in mind that the only job of an annual report is to provide an objective summary of what a business is and what's been going on in it. That's it. As an official SEC document, it isn't there to provide an opinion on a firm's future, and its purpose isn't to tell investors how to analyze the business.

An annual report can tell you a company's profit margins. But they usually won't tell you whether those margins are good or bad.

An annual report can tell you that branding is important, but it can't tell you what the best brand strategy is for a firm.

An annual report can tell you that the customer's experience is a key success factor, but it won't tell you how to evaluate which business will provide the best customer experience.

CEO letters, on the other hand, can say whatever they want, assuming that it doesn't mislead shareholders. Having the best interests of shareholders in mind, good CEOs will use their letter to go in depth into a company's competitive dynamics.

While an annual report can only say what profit margins were, a CEO letter can explain whether margins were good or bad.

While an annual report can only say that brand strength is important, a CEO letter can share a company's brand strategy and explain why it is the best one.

While an annual report can only talk about a company's initiatives to enhance the customer experience, a CEO letter can talk about what they believe consumers care about.

In a sense, an annual report is like a spreadsheet filled with data. It's a bunch of information that's ready for someone to interpret. A well-written CEO letter, on the other hand, is like one person's interpretation of the annual report.

Therefore, always read CEO letters from a company's early history. These will oftentimes contain gems that will help you quickly understand the 80/20 drivers of a business.

REPORT #3:
PERIODS OF FINANCIAL VOLATILITY

Remember, the whole point of studying history is to develop an understanding of why businesses succeed and fail.

The one thing you don't want to do, then, is study a business when it is neither failing nor succeeding, but rather stagnant. If you study a business during those periods, you are unlikely to gain any important insights.

Typically, periods of stagnation are characterized by low levels of financial volatility, little to no sales growth, minimal changes in margins, and lots of capital being paid out to shareholders instead of being reinvested in the business.

Don't focus on studying those periods. You aren't likely to gain important insights.

REPORT #4:
REPORTS OF THE COMPETITION

One of the most basic ideas of investing is that the competitive strength of a company is determined by the strength of the competition.

Think about it. The performance of a company is not determined by its competitive strength. It is determined by its competitive strength relative to that of the competition.

Let's say that I'm operating an oil business that can produce oil at a cost of $50 per barrel. Also, let's say that my competition can only produce oil at $60 per barrel. As of today, I would be the more dominant enterprise since I would be able to undercut the competition. However, if the competition figures out how to produce oil for $40 per barrel, I would start to lose significant market share, even if I'm still able to produce oil at $50 per barrel. The quality of my oil business wouldn't have changed; I'm still able to produce oil at $50 per barrel. But its quality relative to the competition would have decreased since I wouldn't be able to produce oil as cheaply as the competition. Therefore, you cannot understand how competitive one business is unless you understand how competitive the competition is.

Since understanding the competition is so important, you would expect investors to be relentless about understanding it. You would expect McDonald's investors to not only thoroughly read McDonald's annual reports, but also to read Chipotle's annual reports. Why? McDonald's competitive strength depends on Chipotle's competitive strength. Thus, to assess McDonald's competitive strength, you must read Chipotle's annual reports.

But many people rarely do that. In particular, retail investors don't. They oftentimes say, "I read Exxon Mobil's annual report, and I saw that the margins were large and that the sales figures were growing. Thus, it's a great company." Yet, they conclude that Exxon Mobil is a sound company without doing any research at all on BP.

Of course, that wouldn't be a sound conclusion to make. It's not possible to conclude whether Exxon Mobil is strong or weak without studying BP. The competitive strength of a company is simply not determined by its competitive strength. It's determined by its competitive strength relative to the competition.

Therefore, study the competition just as well as the company you want to invest in. If you haven't studied the competitive strength of the competition, you haven't studied the competitive strength of your own company.

Average investors spend time studying what's going on in the markets.

Outlier Investors spend time studying what has happened in the markets.

The Problem of the Annual Report

In the past two years, I've read a little over a dozen books about marketing. My initial purpose in reading those books was to learn how to market the books I've been writing.

But what I've learned is that reading those marketing books was one of the best things I did to make better investment decisions.

A couple of months ago, I felt like learning about a company that I hadn't yet heard of. So, I grabbed a list of random companies, and I randomly picked one of the publicly traded ones on the list. That company happened to be a small restaurant ("The Restaurant") that did a couple of billion dollars in revenue per year.

Moreover, I picked an annual report that was almost 10 years old. This was intentional. Reading an old annual report would allow me to test how well I understand a business. Here is how. After reading an old annual report, I could ask myself, "How much more successful or unsuccessful do I think this business will be in a few years?" After answering the question, I could then check my answer against recent annual reports. This process would allow me to see whether I'm good at predicting businesses.

So, I started to read through the old annual report to make a prediction.

I first looked through the company's financial history to get a sense of what's been going on in the business.

Sales were growing at a modest rate, at about 4%-5% per year. In my opinion, those figures weren't necessarily impressive. Since it was a small player in a big market, I would have expected it to grow quicker. After all, growing quickly in a small market is a sign that a company can take away market share from the incumbents. On the other hand, if such a company isn't growing quickly, it likely means that it's not going to take significant share from incumbents, indicating that it doesn't have a competitive business model.

However, I decided to dig deeper. I remembered the lesson in the chapter called "The Second Layer of Competence," and I knew that I shouldn't simply extrapolate the past into the future. I shouldn't assume that the company will grow slowly in the future because it had a history of growing slowly. Instead, I knew that I had to look at the firm's second-layer drivers to understand its future.

I knew that marketing was a critical driver of a restaurant's sales and customer acquisition efforts. So, I decided to see what the annual report said about the company's marketing efforts.

In that section of the annual report, the company announced that it was changing its marketing strategy to improve store traffic, customer loyalty, and sales growth.

Hearing that the company was improving its marketing strategy made me optimistic about the company. It sounded like the company had a great management team. They noticed that sales growth wasn't phenomenal, so they were working towards fixing the problem. Moreover, assuming that (i) The Restaurant's concept was competitive and that (ii) the only issue involved promoting The Restaurant's concept, it sounded like the management was addressing the right problems in the business.

But as I read deeper, I knew that the company's marketing strategy was bound to fail.

One major red flag was that the company was investing more in direct response marketing than in brand marketing.

For those who don't know, marketing efforts fall into two

categories: direct response marketing and brand marketing.[5] Direct response campaigns attempt to get consumers to take an immediate action, such as signing up for an email list or visiting a location. Brand marketing campaigns, on the other hand, don't attempt to get customers to take any action. Instead, the goal of a brand marketing campaign is to help the consumer become familiar with the brand. For example, McDonald's doesn't expect you to suddenly visit its restaurant after you see a TV ad for it. Instead, it wants you to become familiar with McDonalds's brand so that it comes to the top of your mind in the future.

To grow long-term sales, I knew that the company should be focusing on brand advertising.

The reason I knew that was due to a lesson I learned in a book about McDonald's and branding. It explained that part of McDonald's strength comes from its investments in its logo. McDonald's has spent billions of dollars making the iconic golden arches known to consumers. As a result, consumers can recognize the McDonald's logo faster than that of its competitors. So, if there are 5 restaurants next to each other, consumers are likely to notice the McDonald's sign before that of competitors. That ultimately makes consumers far more likely to choose McDonald's.

Moreover, I knew that direct response marketing tends to be a less effective strategy for growing sales over the long term. One of the books I had read, for example, highlighted that price promotions, a form of direct response marketing, "does not affect ongoing [buying] propensity and does not have favorable long-term effects." In fact, another book—one that I was reading while writing this chapter—further reinforced this belief. The authors conducted an analysis of ads in the IPA Effectiveness Databank, a dataset of successful ad campaigns. What they found is that brand campaigns were far more effective at increasing market share than direct response campaigns.

---

5   There is also a third category called brand response campaigns. But, for simplicity, I'm ignoring them.

Brand campaigns are more effective than direct response campaigns

Percent (%) of companies reporting large growth in market share over campaign duration (years)

Source: The Long and the Short of It

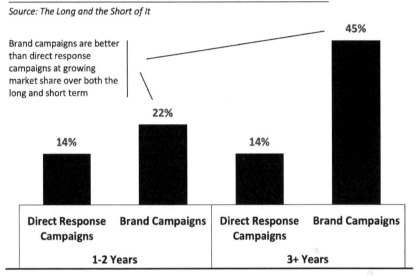

Brand campaigns are better than direct response campaigns at growing market share over both the long and short term

45%

22%

14%

14%

Direct Response Campaigns	Brand Campaigns	Direct Response Campaigns	Brand Campaigns
1-2 Years		3+ Years	

In essence, I knew that focusing on brand marketing over direct response marketing was critical for The Restaurant. After all, the McDonald's and Starbucks of the world build a sustainable competitive advantage by building a strong brand. So, if The Restaurant had an excellent management team—one that is relentless about building its competitive advantage—they would focus on building a brand.

Yet, The Restaurant that I was reading about was doing the opposite. The company directly stated that it was reducing its reliance on brand marketing campaigns and focusing more on direct response campaigns.

What was even more concerning was the quality of the company's brand marketing campaigns.

One of the things I learned from reading marketing books was that marketing messages must be clear in order to be effective.

This was actually one of the main ideas from Donald Miller's *Building A Story Brand*. He correctly points out that ads need to be clear to work.

Logically, that makes sense.

If the call to action is unclear, consumers won't perform it.

If a logo isn't clearly in an ad, consumers won't become familiar with it.

If the message of an ad is unclear, consumers won't remember it.

The Restaurant posted many of their TV ads—one of the main types of ads the company used for brand marketing—on YouTube. After watching many of their ads, I was a little bit shocked that the company ran them because they were unclear.

For one thing, it was very difficult to tell which company was running the ads in the first place. In one ad, for example, The Restaurant's name was simply in tiny letters in the bottom corner of the ad. No one is realistically going to notice that. In other instances, the brand's name and logo were dominated by other things in the ad, making it nearly impossible for consumers to know which company was running the ad.

Of course, that isn't good. Imagine sending a love letter to start a relationship without saying who you are. In that case, the recipient would be able to read your love letter, but they wouldn't be able to get in touch with you. That was exactly what The Restaurant was doing. It was running ads for consumers to build a relationship with it without the brand name and logo appearing prominently in the ad. So, the consumers could see the nice video clips of food in the ad, but they weren't shown which restaurant actually had the nice food. As a result, the chance that the ads were increasing the probability that consumers would visit The Restaurant was zero.

At this point, I hadn't yet looked into everything that's important in evaluating a restaurant. After all, marketing and branding are not the only factors that determine a restaurant's long-term success.

However, I felt that this restaurant had a low chance of growing its sales over time. A business needs intelligent marketing to grow sales. The Restaurant simply didn't have that. Moreover, I had a feeling that its competitive advantage would weaken over time. The Restaurant wasn't establishing its brand in the minds of consumers, while its competitors were doing so. As a result, I knew that the restaurant would slowly weaken over time, relative to the competition.

Within reason, my prediction was correct. After the marketing strategy was implemented, sales started to shrink to the low single digit range. Specifically, they shrank in 75% of the following quarters till Covid-19.

In my shoes, however, most people wouldn't have predicted that The Restaurant's sales would start to fall. If anything, they would have thought that sales would increase. After all, sales had been consistently growing every quarter since its IPO. Moreover, the management team themselves said that the marketing strategy changes would "drive comparable restaurant sales growth" and drive "immediate increases in store traffic."

But I was able to get a more accurate picture of the company's future by reading books—not just annual reports. Several books and studies on marketing taught me that relying on direct response marketing wouldn't build the company's competitive advantage. Moreover, several books made me aware that a relatively unknown brand can't grow unless its marketing campaigns are clear. And when I saw that all of The Restaurant's brand campaigns—which were being used less frequently—were unclear, I knew that the company's brand wouldn't grow.

That illustrates an important investing lesson: only reading annual reports isn't enough to understand whether a business will succeed or fail.

Just think about it.

At the end of the day, Wall Street professionals are finance people. Most of them majored in finance.

They spend much of their time learning how to build financial models in Excel.

And they spend a lot of time analyzing how headwinds and tailwinds will impact quarterly margins and sales growth.

Companies know that Wall Street cares about the numbers. That's what grabs their attention and gets them excited to invest in companies. So, companies, investor relations departments, and management teams feed Wall Street with financial figures.

For example, Gail Kelly, the former CEO of Westpac, an Australian bank, shares that she started to focus on communicating financial figures to Wall Street because that's what they liked:

> I found that my language with our investors wasn't resonating because I spoke the customer's language. I wasn't doing enough to speak the language of banking... The feedback I'd get from investors was 'She's obviously strong on the soft stuff, but it's good she's got a CFO who knows the numbers.' It used to drive me mad... So, I changed. I didn't shift what I focused on. But I shifted my language with investors and started to include a lot of numbers in my answers.

Since companies focus on communicating financial figures to Wall Street, their coverage of important, non-financial factors—marketing strategies, product innovations, and distribution strength—can be shallow.

Take Coca-Cola as an example. If you download Coca-Cola's 2021 annual report from its website, you'll get a 183-page pdf file. You would expect that at least one of those pages would be devoted to marketing. After all, Coca-Cola is a brand. Brands are driven by marketing. Yet, out of those 183 pages, less than one quarter of a page is devoted to the "Promotional and Marketing Programs Section." The Restaurant that I was analyzing had a much more thorough marketing section, and it didn't even have a strong brand.

However, just because annual reports don't always talk about important, non-financial factors doesn't mean that you don't need to understand them. You will likely incorrectly assess the long-term competitive strength of a business if you don't fully understand them. In fact, that's what happened to some investors in The Restaurant. They didn't understand the basics of how marketing causes brands to grow and shrink. So, they overlooked many red flags in The Restaurant's marketing strategy. Consequently, they assumed that it would continue to grow because that was the trend, even though it was likely to decline.

Outlier Investors have a way of coping with the weakness of annual reports, earnings transcripts, and quarterly reports: they supplement their research with other sources of information.

Consider Ted Weschler, one of Warren Buffett's portfolio managers. When he researches businesses, he doesn't only read annual reports, earnings transcripts, and quarterly reports—the financial documents that most investors read. Instead, he said that he spends half of his day reading random things:

> [My] day job is reading, and I spend the vast majority of my day reading. I try to make half of that reading random things like newspapers and trade periodicals.

Or consider Warren Buffett. He doesn't just read annual reports and earnings transcripts. He reads everything:

> I just read and read and read. I probably read 5-6 hours a day... I read five daily newspapers. I read a fair number of magazines. I read 10-K's. I read annual reports, and I read a lot of other things, too... I love reading biographies, for example.

In fact, CNBC journalist Becky Quick once asked Warren Buffett about his research process for his Bank of America investment. In particular, she asked him about how he first learned about the company. In response, Buffett shared two key things. First, as expected, he read Bank of America's annual report: "I probably read [Bank of America's] annual report every year for 50 years." Second, he said that he previously read a book called *Biography of a Bank*. In other words, he supplemented his knowledge from Bank of America's annual report with a book about banks, something that most investors wouldn't do before investing in a bank.

If anything, it makes perfect sense to research businesses by going beyond reading annual reports and earnings transcripts. Morgan Housel, the author of *The Psychology of Money*, once said that "Your personal experiences with money make up maybe 0.00000001% of what's happened in the world, but maybe 80% of how you think the world works." The same concept really applies to investing. Annual reports, earnings transcripts, and quarterly reports probably represent 20% of everything that's happened in the business world, but 80% of most investors' research efforts. Smart investors recognize that. So, they broaden their research efforts. They actively read things that aren't just annual reports—like books, periodicals, studies, magazines, biographies, interviews, and more.

However, there are a few problems. As the "Follow the 80% Past Rule" chapter claimed, Outlier Investors have a significant advantage over retail investors; they invest for a living, so they could devote all their time to reading everything in their sight. For example, Todd Combs, one of Warren Buffett's portfolio managers, literally spends his entire day reading:

> I get in [to the office at] around seven or eight, and I read until about seven or eight at night. And I go home and see my family, and then I'll read for another hour or two in bed at night.

Most people cannot do that, frankly. Of course, most retail investors can't physically read that much because they have day jobs. But the same is true for many professional investors as well. They have many responsibilities not related to reading about companies. They have meetings to go to, models to build, people to manage, investors to deal with, and reports to write. So, even most professional investors can't devote 8 to 14 hours a day to reading.

A second problem is that there is so much information out there. Even if you could read 14 hours a day, you wouldn't be able to read all the information about even one subject. Just imagine trying to read everything about Coca-Cola. You would have to go through dozens and dozens of books about branding, tens of biographies and articles about Coca-Cola executives, dozens and dozens of annual reports about its financial performance, thousands of articles about Coca-Cola's business model, and thousands of journal articles about branding. You can't read all that. Virtually no one can. To conduct research effectively, then, you must be able to distinguish between what is important to read and what is not. If you can't, you'll simply end up reading everything in sight—which will waste enormous amounts of time.

To be a successful investor, then, you have to be able to overcome those two problems. Since you can't read all day, you must learn how to research a business as efficiently as possible. Moreover, since you can't read everything, you must learn how to prioritize your research efforts.

To help you overcome those challenges, I'm about to share a principle for being as efficient as possible when researching a business. What is this principle? It's called "read what's important, not what's relevant."

READ WHAT'S IMPORTANT, NOT WHAT'S RELEVANT

I'm a writer. And writers aren't designers. That means I've always needed to hire graphic designers to create book covers.

When I first started writing, I would only hire entry-level designers. They were affordable, and they could get the job done. At the time, there wasn't a need to hire a world-class designer. I was writing books on investing because I liked to—not because I wanted to hit the bestseller lists.

But, over time, my objectives started to change.

When I was 17, I wrote my third book. It was about the basics of financial statements and the discounted cash flow model. Although I didn't care much about the sales of my first two books, that wasn't the case with my third book; I wanted this book to sell well. To help it sell, I hired a better cover designer. That worked. My third book, *Buffett's 2-Step Stock Market Strategy,* ended up selling over 20,000 copies to date, ten times more than my second book (which frankly wasn't very good).

That got me thinking. I sold more copies partially because I hired a better cover designer. What would happen if I hired the best designer I could find?

So that's what I did.

I screened through at least one hundred of the best cover designers I could find, and I found one person who stood out above all the rest. His designs were much more creative, and he had far better work experience. So, I hired him for $1,200.

A few weeks later, I got the covers. But I didn't really like them. They just weren't appealing. It didn't look like any of them would be a bestseller. However, my designer assured me that those were only first drafts. He made some changes, and he sent them back to me a few weeks later. They didn't show much improvement, so I decided to end the project early.[6]

Out of $1,200, I decided to try and design a cover myself.

The first five I designed turned out poorly. That was expected, of course. It was my first time using Photoshop.

So, I tried again. I designed a couple dozen more covers. But none of them showed any improvement. In fact, they were so bad that I could have paid a random designer $5, and they would have done a better job than me.

That made me realize that I didn't know anything about design. So, I decided to teach myself about it. For several weeks, I would consume everything I could about graphic design. I watched

---

6   In hindsight, I realized that it wasn't the graphic designer's fault that the designs were bad. It was me being a bad leader.

interviews of countless graphic designers. I looked through design inspiration books. I took notes on important lessons I was learning.

And when I started designing covers again, I applied all the important lessons I learned. For a couple of weeks, I spent every day designing covers. I would often wake up at 5:30 am and design covers till 10:30 pm.

I still couldn't create a good cover despite spending countless hours learning about design and implementing the lessons I had learned.

At this point, I was contemplating whether to just hire another designer, when suddenly, I became a very lucky individual.

In my free time, I was studying Apple's success story to learn what made consumers love its product, when a guy named Dieter Rams was mentioned. I didn't recognize the name, so I looked him up.

I learned that Dieter Rams had one of the most impressive track records in industrial design. Most notably, his designs greatly inspired the design of the iPhone, one of the best designed products of the century. In fact, Jony Ive, the former Chief Design Officer of Apple, has stated that he frequently looks to his work for inspiration. If Apple's Chief Design Officer looks up to Dieter Rams, I knew that he was probably one of the best industrial designers in the world. Moreover, if there was anyone who could teach me design, I knew that it would be him.

I saw that he wrote a book on design called *Dieter Rams: 10 Principles for Good Design*. I wanted to learn the ideas in the book right away, and I didn't want to wait two days for Amazon to ship it. So, I pulled up a summary of it.

In no more than 5 minutes of reading a summary of his book, his design principles instantly made sense to me. They were, by far, the best ideas that I've ever read on design. For some reason, you could just tell that Dieter Rams got to the core of what makes good design.

So, I went right to work and applied his principles to design a new book cover.

Dieter Rams said that "good design is as little design as possible" (i.e. simple). So, I made my cover as simple as possible.

Rams said that "good design is innovative." So, I made the cover as innovative as I could.

Rams said that "good design makes a product understandable." So, I made sure that the cover helped readers understand what my book is about.

In the end, the very first cover concept I designed after reading his design principles was by far my favorite one. In fact, I liked it more than the covers I saw many professional cover designers making for their clients. So, I used that design as the cover for this book.[7]

My experience learning about design taught me an important lesson about how to learn efficiently: information sources with important insights aren't necessarily those that feel relevant.

Naturally, our minds look for solutions that sound relevant. We saw this with Coca-Cola at the beginning of this book. People buy drinks to feel happy. Therefore, the drink that a consumer is most likely to buy is the one that's associated with happiness; that product will seem like the most relevant solution to the customer's problems.

In the same way, I had looked for the "solution" that sounded relevant. When learning about design, my goal was to make a good book cover. So, who did I think were the most relevant people to learn from? Book cover designers and graphic designers.

But the problem was that it wasn't efficient to learn from them. I spent hours and hours learning from them and implementing their lessons. Yet, I made virtually no advancements in my ability to make a good book cover.

---

7   Technically, this ending isn't correct. After the content of this book was finalized (i.e. once major structural changes can't be made), I found a remarkable cover designer who was worthy of hiring. I paid him $3,000, and I changed my leadership style by giving him lots of autonomy to do his job. In the end, he created a cover that was better than mine. So, his cover is on this book—not mine. Nonetheless, this story still illustrates an important lesson about learning because it allowed me to develop a cover that I liked better than what most designers would have created.

On the other hand, it was incredibly efficient to learn from Dieter Rams. I had spent literally 5 minutes reading a summary of his book, and I had all the important insights I needed to design a cover.

However, I could not find him very easily, even though he was the best person to learn from. (In fact, I learned about him accidentally when trying to learn about Apple).

The reason that I didn't come across him easily is that he didn't sound like a relevant information source. My mind was looking to learn from graphic designers and book cover designers. But Dieter Rams wasn't known as a book cover designer or a graphic designer. He was an industrial designer. He made things like "clocks, radios, [and] calculators." Therefore, I could have been Googling "book cover design principles" all day, but I wouldn't have come across Dieter Rams, the best person to learn design from.

The same thing happens to investors all the time. Consider The Restaurant from the beginning of this chapter.

Most investors would have researched The Restaurant by reading its recent annual reports and earnings transcripts. After all, those information sources sound relevant to making an investment decision in The Restaurant.

However, it wouldn't have been an efficient way to research The Restaurant. You could have spent hours and hours reading its annual reports, earnings transcripts, and quarterly reports, but you wouldn't have understood how its competitive strength would evolve. The Restaurant's annual report wouldn't have told you that brand marketing is more important than direct response marketing for a restaurant. You would have had to read a book about marketing to learn that. Similarly, its annual report couldn't have told you that the company's ads were ineffective at communicating its marketing messages to customers, making it nearly impossible for the company to grow over the long term. No management team is going to write, "our marketing campaigns significantly underperform the competition" in their annual report. To learn that, you would have had to go to YouTube and research the kinds of campaigns it was running.

In fact, one of the most efficient ways to learn about The Restaurant wouldn't have involved studying it. Instead, it would have involved studying Coca-Cola—an information source that sounds irrelevant. Researching Coca-Cola would have provided invaluable insights into what causes brands to grow and succeed. For example, reading one of the studies that I cited in the chapter called "No One Understand Coca-Cola" would have told you that being associated with something positive—or happiness in the case of Coca-Cola—is important for a brand to grow. Reading a good article on Coca-Cola would have told you what made their marketing campaigns better than their competitors, allowing you to understand what makes a good marketing campaign. Reading a good book on Coca-Cola would have probably told you whether brand marketing or direct response marketing mainly propels brand growth.

You could then have used those insights to evaluate The Restaurant. After learning that Coca-Cola became strong because it associated itself with something positive, you could have asked yourself, "is The Restaurant associating itself with something positive?" If not, it may have been a sign that you shouldn't have confidence in it over the long term—even though it had a track record of growing sales. After learning what made Coca-Cola's marketing campaigns so successful, you could have asked yourself, "are The Restaurant's campaigns similar in quality?" If not, you would have learned that the probability of its brand being established in the minds of more consumers over time was low. After learning that brand marketing is critical for growing long-term market share, you could have asked yourself, "is The Restaurant relying more on brand marketing in the future?" Doing so would have allowed you to simply predict its future.

To summarize, reading relevant sources of information—such as The Restaurant's annual and quarterly reports—wouldn't have provided all the information you needed to know to make an intelligent investment decision. It would have told you that the company was relying on less brand marketing, but not whether that was going to help the brand over the long term. Similarly, reading The Restaurant's annual reports would have told you that a large portion of its marketing budget was spent on TV ads. But it wouldn't have told you whether those ads were clearly communicating the brand's message.

Conversely, reading irrelevant sources of information—such as articles, books, and studies about Coca-Cola—would have greatly helped you make an investment decision in the restaurant. It would have provided you with the specific steps that Coca-Cola took to grow its brand. Then, you would have been able to determine whether The Restaurant was taking similar steps or different ones.

But very few investors would have sought to learn about Coca-Cola to predict The Restaurant's future. On the surface, reading information sources about Coca-Cola doesn't seem relevant at all. After all, Coca-Cola and The Restaurant don't operate in the same niche. The Restaurant is a restaurant, and Coca-Cola is a beverage. In fact, many would say, "How could learning about soft drinks teach me anything about a restaurant? I would simply be much better off reading the annual report of The Restaurant to learn about it."

The reason people would have said that is that they like to gather research materials based on what sounds relevant.

If an investor is analyzing a software company, they are going to read everything about that company. They are going to read the annual reports of all software companies, which seem relevant to making an investment decision in a software company.

They are going to read about successful CEOs in the software industry. Studying software CEOs sounds relevant to making an investment in a software company.

And they are going to read stock analysts' opinions on the software industry. Learning about analysts' opinions on the software industry sounds relevant to making an investment decision in the software space.

In a sense, most people ask themselves two questions to decide what to read:

1. What company and industry am I potentially investing in?

2. What research is available on that company or industry?

Their mindset is to obtain research about Amazon if they are investing in Amazon, and to obtain research on software if they are investing in software.

But that's not the right mindset to have. You don't want to be reading something because it sounds relevant. You don't to be reading something that has "software" in its title merely because you are investing in a software company.

Instead, you should only read an information source if you believe that it will deliver high-quality insight efficiently. Whether something sounds relevant should be out of the question.

Let's continue with the software company example.

To efficiently make an intelligent investment decision in a software company, you might need to know what kind of culture makes software companies successful over the long term. In that case, studying the culture of one of the most innovative companies of our times—Tesla—would be important to understanding what are the characteristics of a culture that can produce innovative products. To most people, studying Tesla's culture might sound irrelevant to making an investment decision in a software company. But it would be important and efficient since being successful in software requires a culture that fosters innovation.

Or you might need to understand what makes consumers like one product over another. Reading the annual report of a software company probably won't tell you that, even though it seems relevant to investing in a software company. You could read ten annual reports and still not understand a thing about consumer behavior. That's inefficient. Instead, it would be far more efficient to learn about consumer behavior by watching interviews of people like Steve Jobs, who was a master at understanding consumer behavior.

Of course, studying Steve Jobs sounds irrelevant to making an investment in a random software company. But it would efficiently give you insights into consumer behavior.

To research a stock efficiently, you want to ask yourself a different set of questions:

1. What do I need to know?

2. What's the best way to obtain that knowledge?

Both of those questions help make your research process more efficient.

The first question defines the scope of your research. At the end of the day, you can't learn every detail about a company. There are hundreds and hundreds of factors that can influence the success of a company. But by first asking yourself "what do I really need to know about this company to make an intelligent investment," you are narrowing the scope of your research to the 20% of factors that produce 80% of the results. In effect, you are limiting your research to only the pieces of information that you need. That saves a lot of time.

The second question allows you identify the fastest way to find "what you really need to know about the company." When you ask yourself the second question, you are taking the time to think about the most efficient method to research a company. It makes you think, "is it better for me to read an annual report about this company or a book about another industry? Is it better for me to do more research into The Restaurant or to learn a little bit about Coca-Cola?" In the end, answering the second question helps you avoid reading "relevant" information sources that aren't going to help you learn about a business in an efficient manner, and it helps you identify "irrelevant" research materials that are actually valuable.

In fact, I was able to predict The Restaurant's future very efficiently by following those two steps.

I first asked myself, "what do I need to know to predict The Restaurant's future?" Among several factors, I knew that marketing was important. Asking that question greatly narrowed my research scope. I went from having to assess every possible factor that could impact the company to at least starting with assessing the marketing strategy. I went from reading everything that could possibly impact a restaurant's success—inflation, interest rates, supply chain issues, management changes—to at least starting with learning about the company's marketing strategy. That, of course, reduced my research time significantly.

I then asked myself, "what is the best way to learn about the company's marketing strategy?" Asking myself that question made me realize that I needed to go directly to the "Advertising and Marketing" section of the annual report. In other words, I knew that I didn't need to read the earnings transcript, a news article, or an industry report at the moment. I just needed to read a couple of paragraphs about marketing that were in the annual report. This also reduced my research time significantly.

In the end, it took no more than ten minutes to conclude that the business wasn't a good investment. Just by asking myself "what do I need to know" and "how do I learn about it," I was able to quickly determine that the company didn't have a sound business strategy.

Of course, I had a slight advantage. I had some general background knowledge on branding. Most people reading this—even some professional stock analysts who analyze brands—probably don't.

Therefore, you would have answered the questions differently.

Overall, your response to the first question ("what do I need to know") would have been similar to mine. Most people know that marketing is an important driver of a restaurant's success. Therefore, most people would recognize that they "need to know" and assess what a restaurant's future brand strength will be before investing in one. Of course, marketing and branding are not the only things you would have needed to analyze, but they would have been major factors.

However, your response to the second question would have been different.

Before analyzing The Restaurant, I studied what makes a good and bad brand. You likely haven't. That means you would need to first learn how to analyze a brand, and your first step would not be to actually analyze The Restaurant's brand. Your answer to the second question shouldn't be to go to the "Advertising and Marketing" section of the company's annual report. It would only tell you what marketing decisions the company is making. But that wouldn't be useful. Since you don't know much about branding, you wouldn't be able to tell whether those decisions are good or bad. So, you wouldn't make much progress towards assessing the long-term trajectory of the company by reading its annual report.

Instead, it would be far more efficient, in your case, to first learn how to evaluate a brand. For example, you could listen to an interview where Phil Knight, the founder of Nike, explains how he built a stronger brand than Adidas. Or reading a good book on Coca-Cola's brand strategy would help you understand what a good brand strategy looks like. Those pieces of information would provide you with foundational knowledge to assess The Restaurant's brand strategy, allowing you to understand whether it would grow or shrink in the future.

Average investors read what's relevant.

Outliers read what's important.

OUTLIER RISK MANAGEMENT STRATEGIES

Not Just a Margin of Safety

July 1st, 1991

On July 1st, 1991, there was a major life insurance company called Mutual Benefit.

Mutual Benefit ran a highly successful operation. According to one news source, Mutual Benefit "was seen as a conservative, blue-chip company" that acquired over $13.8 billion in assets, making it the nation's 18th largest life insurance company.

It was viewed as one of the safest life insurance companies in the industry. A.M. Best Co., a leading insurance rating agency, rated Mutual Benefit as an A+, which meant that Mutual Benefit had a "superior ability to meet their ongoing insurance obligations." When rating agencies like A.M. Best Co. rate insurance companies, they consider many factors such as trends in an insurer's financials, expected payouts, and capital levels. To have achieved an A+ rating, Mutual Benefit had to be sound in all those areas.

Moreover, most of Mutual Benefit's assets were in relatively safe investments. At the time, it had about 40% of its investment portfolio in commercial mortgages and real estate. Though many insurance experts would claim that a 40% concentration in one asset class was large, it didn't ring too many alarms because real estate was generally not considered a very risky asset class.

July 16th, 1991

On July 16th, 1991, the *Los Angeles Times* published an article with the following headline: "Mutual Benefit Insurance Fails After Run on Assets: It is the largest [of] such collapses in the U.S." By July 16th, the company collapsed, it lost its A+ rating, and the government had to take control of it to prevent a larger financial crisis from ensuing.

Now, how could a company go from being a major blue-chip insurance company to being essentially insolvent in just a couple of weeks?

The main reason was an improper management of tail risks (risk that occur infrequently but have high consequences when they do).[8] Shortly before July 1991, several other insurance companies collapsed due to poor investments in junk bonds. These were also fairly large names, such as Executive Life and First Capital. Seeing large insurance companies collapse made people fearful. In particular, policyholders of Mutual Benefit became worried that Mutual Benefit would collapse as well. Rationally, then, policyholders of Mutual Benefit played it safe. Not wanting to wait for Mutual Benefit to collapse, they cashed out their life insurance policies (Just like how you can withdraw money from a bank, you can cash in or "withdraw" life insurance policies). As a result, Mutual Benefit had to pay out an unexpectedly large amount of cash—far more than it had on hand. Consequently, it couldn't pay the people it owed money to, causing it to go bankrupt.

Every well-run insurance company knows that unexpected tail risks occur. Sometimes there are unexpected major natural disasters, which significantly increase insurers' claims. For example, the insurance industry had to pay about $41.1 billion to policyholders

---

8   To those who aren't familiar with insurance, here is a simplified explanation: Insurance companies collect premiums ("revenues") from customers. In exchange, they agree to pay out claims (expenses) to policyholders (customers) when certain circumstances are met (such as a car crash). Insurance companies make money on the difference between the premiums and claims, plus any gains from investing the premiums.

for damages caused by Hurricane Katrina. Other times, unexpected terrorist attacks occur, which lead to significant claims. That happened during 9/11, which caused some of the largest property losses at the time.

Although insurers know that unexpected tail risks will occur, they don't know when they will occur. At the same time, however, they must be prepared to pay out a large sum of money when unexpected tail risks occur.

So, what the most intelligent and competitive insurance businesses do is always maintain a large enough balance of liquid assets—such as cash—to be able to pay out claims when the unexpected occurs. In particular, the most pristine insurance companies ensure that they can deal with the most severe tail risks. Take Berkshire Hathaway's insurance operation, which owns major insurers like Geico, as an example. To ensure that they can pay out claims under "worst-case scenario" circumstances, Berkshire Hathaway has pledged to keep a whopping $30 billion cash balance at all times. So, even under severe conditions, they will always have enough cash to pay out claims.

But what's interesting is that Mutual Benefit didn't do that. They didn't prepare for a worst-case scenario. Actually, they didn't have much cash at all to withstand any crisis. One expert on the Mutual Benefit crisis, Murray Becker, noted that "there was almost a total lack of liquidity." Therefore, Mutual Benefit did not properly manage tail risks.

That should surprise you.

If you think about it, insurance companies are supposed to be some of the best risk managers. Actually, their entire business model is to manage risk. For example, whenever you drive a car, you are taking on risk. Your car might get damaged, which could cause several thousand dollars in damages. To manage the risk (and be in compliance with state laws), most people buy auto insurance. What auto insurance does is transfer the risk to the insurance company. In other words, the insurance company, instead of the individual, takes on that risk. As a result, the insurance company becomes obligated to pay out claims when a car crash occurs. The way they make money, then, is by ensuring that they don't take on too much risk. If they take on too much risk (i.e. more cars crash than expected), then they become obligated to pay more claims, hurting profits. If they minimize the risks they take, they minimize claims and maximize profits. Thus, an insurer's main job is to manage risk.

That may make the Mutual Benefit situation surprising to some individuals; they dramatically failed at their one job, which is to manage risk.

Cases like Mutual Benefit's aren't uncommon, however. Many insurance companies have difficulties managing highly improbable, yet highly impactful risks. For example, during a recent Berkshire Hathaway annual meeting, Warren Buffett noted that three of the largest insurance companies "came close to extinction in the last 30 years" due to highly improbable, yet highly impactful risks. Two of those three companies needed to make a deal with Berkshire Hathaway to help avoid extinction.

Now, if insurance companies—risk management experts—often fail to manage risk, how good do you think investors—some of whom are perceived as gamblers—manage risk? Not very well.

Consider the story of Nick Leeson. Leeson was an incredibly successful trader at Barings Bank's Singapore trading floor. Although he never attended college, he managed to become the general manager of the trading division by age 28. On top of his career accomplishments, he was worth big money for Barings. Reports state that he was so successful at trading derivatives that he once accounted for over 10% of the entire bank's profits. From a financial standpoint, he was probably one of the bank's most valuable non-executive employees.

After some big wins, however, he started to lose a bit of money. After all, almost every investor has some bad days. Bill Ackman, an Outlier Investor, turned around Canadian Pacific railway and tripled his money in one trade. But he had an unfortunate instance with JCPenney, which we will talk about later. In 1968, Warren Buffett and Charlie Munger returned 77.8% for Berkshire Hathaway shareholders (compared to the S&P 500's return of 11%). However, in 1974, just a few years later, Buffett and Munger significantly underperformed. They lost 48.7%, while the S&P 500 only lost 26.4%. Nick Leeson was in a similar situation. He had a good track record, but he was having a bad day.

At the end of the day, Barings Bank recognized that every trader would lose money at some point. So, like most banks, Barings Bank required traders to report any losses when they occurred. Having traders report losses allowed the bank to keep track of them and ensure that they didn't get too large. (If they got too large, they would end up like Mutual Benefit, without enough cash to pay customers who wanted to withdraw money).

But Nick Leeson chose not to report his losses. After all, it would hurt his reputation if the bank knew that he had lost money. To ensure that the bank didn't find out, he manipulated the books and created a "secret account" that contained all the losses. The "secret account," though, was only a temporary solution. The bank would eventually learn about the losses. But at least it hid the losses temporarily. The time, he hoped, would allow him to make the money back.

One of the ways he attempted to make up the losses was by placing a short straddle on the Nikkei, Tokyo's version of the S&P 500.

A short straddle (as a former finance professor, Mr. Smith, taught me) is an options trading strategy where an individual sells a put and a call option. Recognizing that many readers may not be familiar with options, I won't go into great detail. But what you need to know is that a short straddle is a bet on low volatility.

If the markets aren't volatile and stay at current levels, Nick Leeson makes money.

If the markets go down a lot, Leeson loses money.

If the markets go up a lot, Leeson also loses money.

So, the markets essentially must do nothing for Nick Leeson to make money.

Most investors would consider a short straddle a low-risk bet. On 99% of trading days, the markets don't make much noise. They might blip up or down by a fraction of a percent, but that's about it. Especially since there weren't any major events—such as wars, pandemics, or financial crises—that could cause the markets to move, it was safe to say that the markets wouldn't move a lot. Thus, the chances that he would lose lots of money were fairly small.

So, on the 16th of January, 1995, Nick Leeson decided to initiate a short straddle on the Nikkei, believing that it would be a low-risk way to recover his losses.

Given that this chapter is about risk management, you can probably guess that it didn't go too well.

On the 17th of January, 1995, a major earthquake hit Japan.

The markets tanked.

Nick Leeson lost serious money—accumulating about £827 million or $1.4 billion in total losses.[9]

He knew that Barings Bank couldn't handle those kinds of losses, and he knew that the bank would get mad at him for losing $1.4 billion and manipulating the books.

So, he fled the country.

Before leaving, however, he left Barings Bank a note to say "sorry" for losing $1.4 billion. But the note did matter much because the bank collapsed a couple of days later due to the losses. And, eventually, Nick Leeson was caught in Germany, and went to jail for committing fraud.

Nick Leeson made the same mistake as Mutual Benefit. Mutual Benefit was prepared to handle most crises. However,

---

9   To be historically accurate, Nick Leeson technically made a few more trades after the short straddle on the Nikkei. But the short straddle on the Nikkei is often cited as the main cause of his failure.

it wasn't prepared to manage an unexpected tail risk, a run on assets, which ultimately led to its bankruptcy. Similarly, although Leeson could handle the uncertainties that occurred on 99% of trading days, he wasn't prepared to bear the consequences of one major crisis.

To manage highly improbable yet highly impactful risks, most investors invest with a margin of safety.

For those who don't know, the term margin of safety was initially written about in Benjamin Graham's *The Intelligent Investor*, and popularized by Warren Buffett.

Investing with a margin of safety essentially means leaving some room for error. For example, let's say that you think a stock is worth $45. Not investing with a margin of safety would mean directly purchasing the stock for $45. That obviously wouldn't be a good idea. An unexpected headwind could occur, causing you to earn an inadequate return on investment. Investing with a margin of safety, on the other hand, would involve your purchasing the stock below $45—perhaps at $30. By doing so, you would leave yourself room for error. If a depression occurs that makes the stock's "fair value" only $40, you'll be fine. You would only have paid $30, not $45, for an asset that's worth $40. In other words, you would have bought something that's worth $40 for only $30. That's much better than buying something that's worth $40 for $45.

In a sense, a margin of safety protects investors against unexpected risks.

If an unexpected recession occurs, it doesn't matter because there was some room for error.

If sales growth is lower than expected, it doesn't matter because there was some room for error.

If a product's quality is lower than expected, it doesn't matter because there was some room for error.

Therefore, you always want to invest with a margin of safety. There isn't a reason not to do so. When you invest with a margin of safety, you are limiting your downside. Who wouldn't want that?

However, it can't mitigate tail risks—highly improbable yet highly impactful risks.

Take Dexter Shoe as an example.

In 1993, Warren Buffett acquired a company called Dexter Shoe, a domestic shoe manufacturer.

Dexter Shoe was an incredibly strong business, according to Buffett:

> Dexter, I can assure you, needs no fixing: It is one of the best-managed companies Charlie [Munger] and I have seen in our business lifetimes.

Buffett also forecasted that Dexter Shoe and H.H. Brown, Berkshire Hathaway's other shoe business, would make a total of $85 million in pretax profits in 1994, which was in line with historical trends.

However, in 1999, six years after the acquisition, Dexter Shoe and H.H. Brown reported only $17 million in pretax profits. That's far below the $85 million in pretax profits that Buffett had projected a few years earlier.

From then on, Buffett described Dexter Shoe as a "gruesome mistake" and as "the worst deal that [he has] ever made."

What had happened from 1993 to 1999? Why did profits fall so dramatically? And how did Dexter Shoe go from being "one of the best-managed companies" to being a "gruesome mistake?"

Well, an improbable risk occurred: the industry was offshored. In many foreign countries, minimum wages were far lower than in US markets, where Dexter Shoe operated. That allowed foreign businesses to produce shoes at a far lower cost. As a result, they undercut Dexter Shoe and H.H. Brown, reducing their profits by about 80%.

No reasonable margin of safety would have been able to protect Warren Buffett from the offshoring risk. Think about it. Buffett purchased Dexter Shoe for $433 million. However, its fair value was actually 80% lower than $433 million (or $86.6 million) because Dexter Shoe's profitability fell by roughly 80%.[10] Thus, Buffett would have needed to purchase Dexter Shoe for less than $86.6 million in order to avoid losing money.

Buffett could have purchased Dexter Shoe with a 10% margin of safety, or for $389.7 million. But he would still have overpaid for Dexter Shoe because the business was only worth $86.6 million.

Buffett could have purchased Dexter Shoe with a 25% margin of safety or for $324.75 million. But he would still have overpaid for Dexter Shoe.

Buffett could have purchased Dexter Shoe with a 50% margin of safety or for $216.5 million. But he would still have overpaid.

Thus, even with a large margin of safety, Dexter Shoe would have been a bad investment.

The reason the margin of safety principle couldn't have protected Buffett is simple. A margin of safety can't protect investors against highly improbable, yet highly impactful risks.

In most cases, highly impactful risks can cause a stock to lose most of its long-term value. Dexter Shoe, for example, lost around 80% of its value when the shoe industry was offshored. In Mutual Benefit's case, its business value fell to essentially zero. And in Nick Leeson's case, it resulted in the bankruptcy of a bank.

For an investor to be protected against a highly impactful risk, then, they would need an abnormally large margin of safety. Warren Buffett, for example, would have needed to buy Dexter Shoe with an 80% margin of safety from the price that he paid. Buying

---

10   Note that this is a simplified example that makes several simplified assumptions. For example, it assumes that $433 million was what Buffett thought Dexter Shoe's intrinsic value was. It assumes that Dexter Shoe and H.H. Brown's profitability both fell by 80%, which isn't entirely true. Moreover, it assumes that Dexter Shoe's and H.H. Brown's profitability didn't recover after it fell by 80%. It assumes that Dexter Shoe's intrinsic value declined in proportion to its profitability. It also doesn't account for the fact that Buffett paid for Dexter Shoe with Berkshire Hathaway stock.

Dexter Shoe at 80% below $433 million would have allowed him to purchase it for $86.6 million.

However, you are highly unlikely to find securities trading with that sort of margin of safety. Just think about. Let's say that you think a stock is worth $100. If you buy it with an 80% margin of safety, you would be paying $20 for the stock. You would be buying a stock that's worth $100 for only $20. In other words, you would be buying a stock that you think could go from $20 to $100, which is a 600% increase. So, if you find a stock with an 80% margin of safety, you would be implying that it could go up 600%. However, consistently finding stocks that can go up 600% is not a reasonable expectation. Warren Buffett, for example, was one of the most successful investors, but he has only averaged roughly 20% per year over the long term. Therefore, it is highly unreasonable to expect that you can consistently find stocks with an 80% margin of safety and earn 600% every year.

At the same time, however, it is a problem that most investors can't find stocks with 80% margins of safety. The only way the margin of safety principle can protect investors from highly impactful risks is if the margin of safety is abnormally large. But most investors won't find stocks with such large margins of safety. That means the margin of safety principle cannot protect investors against tail risks—the most dangerous kind of risk.

In fact, within Berkshire Hathaway's insurance business, Warren Buffett recognizes the limitation of the margin of safety principle. Consider this. Buffett has often said that Berkshire Hathaway underwrites insurance with a margin of safety. If Berkshire needs to earn, hypothetically, $10 million in premiums to have a favorable risk-reward trade off, it isn't going to underwrite the policy if the company is only going to earn $10 million and one cent in premiums. In that case, there isn't any room for error. Instead, it will only underwrite the policy if it can earn, hypothetically, $11 million in premiums. Doing so would provide a $1 million cushion.

But that begs an important question: why does Buffett keep a $30 billion cash cushion for his insurance operations? Berkshire Hathaway's insurance companies all underwrite insurance with a margin of safety, so what's the point of the extra cushion? It's to protect Berkshire against tail risks. He knows that merely underwriting insurance with a margin of safety won't protect him when tail risks—pandemics, wars, recessions—occur. When tail risks that cause billions of dollars in damages occur, merely having a $1 million margin of safety isn't going to be enough. The $30 billion cash reserve is what can get Berkshire Hathaway through those kinds of crises.

That same concept applies to investing. You can and should invest with a margin of safety, just like how Buffett knows it is a good idea to underwrite insurance with a margin of safety. But you must realize that merely investing with a margin of safety is not enough. While it can protect you against a majority of risks, it won't protect you from highly impactful risks. A margin of safety could have protected Warren Buffett's investment in Dexter Shoe from losing a few important contracts, but it couldn't have protected him from the entire industry being offshored. A margin of safety could have protected Nick Leeson from slightly higher than expected volatility, but it couldn't have protected him from an earthquake. Thus, if you merely rely on the margin of safety principle to protect yourself from downside risk, you'll leave yourself exposed to highly impactful risks—the most dangerous risks.

To ensure that you don't blow yourself up, then, I'm going to share a method to safely mitigate highly improbable, yet highly impactful risks.

THE BILLION DOLLAR TEST

Many investors buy into companies with sustainable competitive advantages to reduce risk.

As many know, one of the key tenets of Warren Buffett's investment philosophy is to invest in companies with strong competitive advantages—companies that are able to consistently deliver more value to the marketplace than competitors. They are the Coca-Colas and Amazons of the world. All companies with a sustainable competitive advantage have one common characteristic: you can't compete against them.

Logically, most investors favor companies with sustainable competitive advantages. A sustainable competitive advantage reduces the chances of a competitor developing a better product or service. What this means is that they protect a business from the most serious, impactful risk: the competition.

In fact, most prominent investment books advise investors to invest in companies with sustainable competitive advantages. For example, *The Dhandho Investor* by Mohnish Pabrai, *Rule #1 Investing* by Phil Town, *The 5 Rules for Successful Stock Investing* by Pat Dorsey, and my book, *Buffett's 2-Step Stock Market Strategy* all recommend that investors buy stocks with sustainable competitive advantages.

Most books—including my previous one—claim that there are roughly 3-5 types of sustainable competitive advantages, which can be seen in the next graphic.

Generally speaking, those books have recommended that investors invest in companies that have one of those types of sustainable competitive advantages. For example, many books will say, "Coca-Cola has a strong competitive edge due to their brand strength. Therefore, you should look for companies with a strong brand because having a strong brand will mean that it will have a strong edge like Coca-Cola." Similarly, they say, "Facebook is impossible to compete against because it benefits from the network effects. Therefore, you should invest in companies that benefit from the network effects because that company will likely also have an edge."

Now, I don't believe that advice, per se, is bad. There is nothing wrong with advising individuals to invest in companies that have a strong brand or that benefit from the network effects.

Most investors decide whether a company is low-risk based on whether it falls into one of these categories

Competitive advantage	Definition
Strong brand	Firms with strong brands are able to consistently attract more customers than weak brands
Low-cost advantage	Firms with strong brands can consistently undercut competitors
Network effects	The value of a firm's product increases as it gains users, making it hard for competitors to compete
High switching costs	Significant costs customers face when switching to a competitor's product
Intangible assets (excluding brands)	If a company has valuable patents, trademarks, and copyrights, then it can provide a better product and service than competitors

But the problem I've noticed is that they can cause new investors to analyze the competitive strength of a business in a robotic manner.

After reading such books, new investors end up assuming that all strong brands have a strong competitive advantage. They end up assuming that high-switching costs automatically give a firm a strong competitive advantage. And they end up thinking that all low-cost commodity producers have a sustainable competitive advantage.

That's not really the case. Many companies can fall into those categories and still have a weak competitive advantage. In other words, a company can have a strong brand or be a low-cost producer, and at the same time, it can be exposed to highly improbable, yet highly impactful competitive risks.

There are so many examples to consider.

Remember Dexter Shoe? It was "one of the best-managed companies Charlie [Munger] and [Warren Buffett] have seen in [their] business lifetimes" because it had a significant low-cost advantage over the competition. Most people would have said that it had a moat. But it was exposed to a highly improbable, yet highly impactful risk: foreign competition. As mentioned earlier, the entire business ended up being offshored in just a couple of years, and it lost most of its profits.

Or what about JCPenney? JCPenney was an iconic American business. In 1977, it was doing $10 billion in sales every year. In 1994, the magazine *Women's Wear Daily* called JCPenney the "Number One Best Store For Women's Apparel." They were the low-cost apparel company. They had efficient economies of scale. They had one of the strongest brands in America. But highly improbable, yet highly impactful risk occurred. They couldn't stay relevant to consumers, so consumers forgot about them.

How about MySpace? There were very few companies that benefited from network effects more than MySpace. From 2004 to 2009, it was the world's largest social networking site. In 2006, it was visited more often than Google. But they were exposed to a highly impactful risk: Facebook. After Facebook came along, MySpace's competitive advantage eroded in the blink of an eye.

Consider Adidas. In the early 1970s, they dominated the footwear market. They had the most popular brand in the country. And they weren't the leading brand for one or two years, but for 20. They had an incredibly long history of building a strong brand. Most investors couldn't have asked for a better brand. However, Adidas was exposed to a highly impactful risk—a better product and brand, Nike, which was created in 1971. By 1980, Nike had gained more of the market share than Adidas.[11] Of course, Adidas is still around. But its competitive strength was greatly diminished by Nike.

In your lifetime, you will see the competitive positionings of companies weaken. But not just any type of company. You will see market leaders that dominate the competition weaken significantly.

---

11   Nike did struggle for a few years after overtaking Adidas, but it eventually clearly overtook Adidas.

And they will not be regular market leaders. They will be companies that have been dominating the markets for decades—the Amazons and Apples of the world.

A mini "stunt" Warren Buffett made during a Berkshire Hatha-way meeting illustrates this point. He pulled up a list of the 20 larg-est companies in the world measured by market cap. It included big, brand-name companies, many of which people view as being invincible: Apple, Saudi Aramco, JPMorgan Chase, Mastercard, etc. The full list of companies can be seen in the next graphic. Then, Warren Buffett asked the audience a question: "how many of those companies are going to be on the list 30 years from now?" Most people in the audience were thinking that probably most of those companies will be around 30 years from now. They may have told themselves, "I'm not too familiar with LVMH Moet, Taiwan Semi-conductor, and Tencent, so I'm not sure where those companies will be 30 years from now. But I know that companies like Amazon, Mastercard, Alphabet, and Apple are extraordinarily competitive. Therefore, I'm sure that they will be around 30 years from now."

After letting the audience guess, Warren Buffett showed another list. The new list, again, showed the 20 largest companies in the world. However, this time it showed the 20 largest companies from 1989—about 30 years before when the first list was created. The first thing that caught the audience off guard was that none of the 20 companies on the 1989 list were on the 2021 list. In other words, none of the largest companies in 1989 were the largest com-panies in the world 30 years later. Then Buffett told the audience, "I would [have] guessed that very few of you, when I asked you to play the quiz a... few minutes ago, would have put down zero."

The companies on the 1989 list were the Amazons and Apples of the time. Yet none of them made it to the 2021 list. Of course, those companies, such as Exxon Mobil and IBM, are still around. But they are no longer the Amazons and Apples of the world. This vividly illustrates that one day, some of the Amazons and Apples of the world may no longer be the Amazons and Apples of the world.

Placement	Company	Market cap ($)
	Twenty largest companies by market cap—2021	
1	Apple	2.05 T
2	Saudi Aramco	1.92 T
3	Microsoft	1.78 T
4	Amazon	1.56 T
5	Alphabet	1.39 T
6	Facebook	838 B
7	Tencent	752 B
8	Tesla	641 B
9	Alibaba	614 B
10	Berkshire Hathaway	587 B
11	Taiwan Semiconductor	534 B
12	Visa	467 B
13	JP Morgan Chase	464 B
14	Johnson & Johnson	432 B
15	Samsung Electronics	430 B
16	Kweichow Moutai	385 B
17	Walmart	382 B
18	Mastercard	353 B
19	United Health	351 B
20	LVMH Moet	336 B

Twenty largest companies by market cap—1989		
Placement	**Company**	**Market cap ($)**
1	Industrial Bank of Japan	104 B
2	Sumitomo Bank	73 B
3	Fuji Bank	69 B
4	Dai-ichi Kangyo Bank	64 B
5	Exxon Corp	63 B
6	General Electric USA	58 B
7	Tokyo Electric Power	56 B
8	IBM Corp	55 B
9	Toyota Motor Corp	53 B
10	American Tel & Tel	48 B
11	Nomura Securities	46 B
12	Royal Dutch Petroleum	41 B
13	Philip Morris	38 B
14	Nippon Steel	36 B
15	Tokai Bank	35 B
16	Mitsui Bank	34 B
17	Matsushita Elect Ind'l	33 B
18	Kansai Electric Power	33 B
19	Hitachi	32 B
20	Merck & CO	30 B

When investing, you will be analyzing many companies that have a strong competitive advantage today, and many of them will have had a strong competitive advantage for many decades. But you must be able to tell the difference between the ones that will continue to be the Amazons and Apples of the world and the ones that will lose their competitive edge over time. If you can't, you'll likely end up with your own Dexter Shoe one day.

One of the best ways to avoid a Dexter Shoe situation is to follow the Billion Dollar Test. The Billion Dollar Test is a simple rule of thumb that helps you truly understand whether a firm is exposed to highly improbable, yet highly impactful risks.

The rule of thumb states that you should ask yourself one question before buying any stock: if I had a billion dollars, could I overthrow this business? If the answer is yes, then it is likely exposed to highly improbable yet highly impactful competitive threats—even if it is a market leader today. If the answer is no, then there is a good chance that it is immune to highly impactful risks.

The Billion Dollar Test once helped me identify that a company I owned was exposed to a high improbable, yet highly impactful risk. One of the first stocks I had ever invested in was a full-service restaurant. On the surface, it seemed like a decent company. The brand was well-known. You've most likely at least heard of the company. Customers loved the company's food. That made me more confident in the company's long-term trajectory. The financials were phenomenal. There was little debt on the balance sheet. Revenues and profits had about a 10-year history of growth. Margins were expanding. So, I told myself, "what could go wrong?"

Within a few weeks of buying the stock, however, I felt uncomfortable owning it. I knew the business was strong. But I didn't think it was competitive enough. So, I applied The Billion Dollar Test. I asked myself, "Could someone overthrow this restaurant if they really wanted to? Could someone develop a better brand than this restaurant? Could someone obtain better locations?" And I concluded that a smart person could easily do all those things. I knew that an intelligent marketer could develop a better brand.

The restaurant's brand was famous and well-known, but it wasn't strong. Unlike how McDonald's brand makes many consumers choose it over Burger King, this restaurant's brand wasn't making consumers choose it far more often than the competition. Moreover, I didn't believe that the brand's strength would grow in the future. So, I sold the stock.

In hindsight, I am happy I sold the stock. Otherwise, I wouldn't have been able to sleep well every night. I would have been worried that someone would develop a stronger brand and open better locations.

Now, deciding to sell the stock didn't mean I was bearish on the company. Nor did it mean that I thought that the company was bad. In fact, it was a perfectly decent company.

However, the reason I sold it was that it was like Mutual Benefit and Dexter Shoe. The restaurant, Dexter Shoe, and Mutual Benefit all had long track records of being competitive businesses, but they all possessed risks that could blow them up. Simply put, the investment contained risk that I wasn't willing to bear the consequences of.

Before we move on, I want to say that I did not come up with The Billion Dollar test. I do not deserve any credit for it. I learned it from Warren Buffett. In 2003, Warren Buffett gave a speech at the University of Nebraska, where he told students about the Billion Dollar Test:

> Every time I buy a business, I say to myself, 'If I had a billion dollars and [if] I wanted to go and compete with these guys, could I knock them off.'

Outlier Investors never just invest with a margin of safety.

Instead, they invest in businesses that are insulated from tail risks.

Find Hidden Risks

JCPenney was one of America's most successful companies. In 1973, it had over 2,000 locations, and it was doing over $6.2 billion in sales.

The company would attract customers by heavily discounting its merchandise. For example, they would initially price an item at $40. But it wouldn't sell at that price. So, they would then cut the price to $20 the following week. But it still wouldn't sell. So, they would send the customer some $10 coupons and provide some other discounts. And only then, customers would start buying.

By the 2000s, however, its model was no longer working. For one, it was a mall-based retailer. Malls were dying, making it harder to get traffic. On top of that, the brand was "outdated." Moreover, its stores tended to be quite large, making it difficult to generate competitive sales per square foot. In 2006, for example, JCPenney only generated $164 per square foot. By comparison, an incredibly successful business like McDonald's generates about $600 in sales per square foot.

But everyone wasn't bearish on the company. Bill Ackman was one of them.

If you don't know, Bill Ackman is an incredibly successful investor. He started his first hedge fund right after getting an MBA from Harvard Business School, and he grew assets under management from $3 million to $300 million dollars. Though his first hedge fund had to close after a decade due to a poor investment, he later started a second hedge fund: Pershing Capital Management.

At Pershing Square, he developed a reputation for turning around businesses. One of his most successful turnarounds was Canadian Pacific Railway.

Bill Ackman thought that Canadian Pacific "was the worst-run railroad in North America." He wasn't wrong. It had the lowest profit margins. It had the worst industry-specific KPIs. And it had the lowest P/E ratio among the railroads (which Bill Ackman took as a sign that the market didn't like the business).

However, he noticed that the business could be fixed with one simple solution. Just replace the "worst CEO in the railroad industry with the best CEO in the railroad industry." So, that's what he did. He acquired a 14% stake in Canadian Pacific, and he got one of the best railroad CEOs to run Canadian Pacific. After 16 months, Canadian Pacific became one of the most profitable railroads in North America, and the company's stock more than tripled.

Bill Ackman saw JCPenney as a similar type of situation. Replace the CEO. Improve the business. And make some quick money.

Recognizing a buying opportunity during the financial crisis, he quickly executed it. Bill Ackman bought a 16% stake in JCPenney and joined the board of directors.

While looking for a replacement CEO, there was one candidate who consistently stood out: Ron Johnson. His work experiences were just remarkable. Most notably, he was hired by Steve Jobs to create the original design of the Apple Store. (If you've been in an Apple store, you can tell that he has done a fine job). The board agreed that he was a strong candidate, and he was hired.

One of Ron Johnson's turnaround initiatives was to implement a "fair and square pricing strategy," which sought to eliminate JCPenney's discounting strategy. The reason that Ron Johnson wanted to get rid of JCPenney's discounting strategy was that it was inefficient from a cost perspective. Just think about it.

As a heavy discounter, JCPenney would lower the prices of every item at least 2-3 times. They might initially price an item for

$40. It wouldn't sell. Lower it to $25. It still wouldn't sell. Lower it to $10, and it would sell a lot.

However, that process contained a lot of waste. Whenever JCPenney lowered prices, an employee had to change the price signs in the store. That means an employee had to change the signs on every item 2-3 times. That, of course, requires a lot of money. Employees aren't cheap, after all.

So, Ron Johnson came up with a brilliant solution. He suggested that JCPenney shouldn't initially sell items at high prices and then mark them down 2-3 times. Instead, he believed that JCPenney should simply price items at the lower price initially. Then, they wouldn't have to mark down the prices at least 2-3 times. Employees wouldn't have to waste time on price changes. And JCPenney would save money.

So, Ron Johnson rolled out the new pricing strategy across every JCPenney in the USA.

The results were phenomenal—phenomenally poor.

A company's brand sets the expectations for the consumer.

When people think of McDonald's, they expect the food to be cheap.

When people think of Tesla, they expect the cars to be innovative.

When people think of Rolex, they expect the watches to be flashy.

And when people thought of JCPenney, they expected to see a sale. They not only expected the merchandise to be cheap, but they also expected to see the discount that they were getting. They didn't want to see that the item was selling for $10. They wanted to see that it was 75% off and that it was marked down from $40 to $10.

But Ron Johnson stopped the sales. JCPenney was no longer selling an item for $40 and then putting it on sale for $10. They simply had the regular price as $10.

So, consumers stopped showing up.

Sales fell from $17.2 billion in 2011 to $12.9 billion in 2012. JCPenney went from losing $150 million in 2011 to losing almost $1 billion in 2012.

Ron Johnson and Bill Ackman were shocked that sales collapsed. They didn't think that it was possible that the new pricing strategy could cause sales to fall. Moreover, they didn't imagine that sales declines of that magnitude could occur. It just wasn't within the realm of possibilities they imagined.

In the end, Ron Johnson was fired from JCPenney about a year after being hired. Although it took several years for JCPenney to fail after Ron Johnson left, some media outlets ended up referring to him as the man who "killed" JCPenney.

When making decisions, we are sometimes oblivious to the risks involved.

This is one reason why JCPenney lost about 25% of its sales. Ron Johnson, Bill Ackman, and the board of directors all saw the upside of the new pricing strategy: reduced labor costs. However, they were oblivious to the downside: an alienated customer base. They didn't think that it was a possibility that customers would stop shopping if they removed the sales. They only learned that that could occur after they removed the sales.

Being oblivious to important risks is one of the main causes of failure in both business and investing.

Consider the story of Joe Campbell. Joe Campbell, your average individual, initiated a $37,000 short position in KaloBios. (A short position is a bet that the stock will go down). KaloBios was a failed pharmaceutical company. At the time, KaloBios announced that it would shut down operations due to running out of cash. Moreover, they had hired a restructuring firm, Brenner Group, to liquidate the company.

Typically, short positions are exposed to unlimited losses.

When you buy (long) a stock, the worst-case scenario is that the stock goes to zero. In that case, you can't lose more than your investment. If you buy a stock for $5 and if it goes to $0, you lose $5.

Shorting is just the opposite. The worst-case scenario is that the stock goes up. However, in theory, stock prices can go infinitely high. That means you can theoretically lose an infinite amount of money. For example, let's say that you short $5 worth of stock. If that stock goes from $5 to $10,000, you lose $9,995—even though you only shorted $5 worth of stock.

In Joe Campbell's situation, however, the losses appeared limited. Remember, KaloBios just announced that it was liquidating. The value of a liquidating company is only worth the value of its assets less its liabilities. A liquidating company cannot be worth more than that. Why? There is no other way the company can make money for shareholders. Typically, the value of a company is derived from its profitability. The more profits a company makes, the more its stock will be worth. But companies that liquidate seize to make profits for shareholders. So, they are only worth the value of what the company's assets can be sold for, less the debts it must pay back. That's the maximum value of the company. It's limited at that figure, limiting the upside potential of the stock price (and the downside potential of Joe's short).

So, Joe Campbell decided to short the stock. After all, the company was about to shut down, so its situation couldn't get much better. Moreover, his downside was limited. No one would be willing to pay more for the stock than its liquidation value, so there was a limit to how much the stock could increase.

But he overlooked one risk—that someone might try to step in and turn the company around (like Bill Ackman).

That's exactly what happened.

Martin Shkreli, a hedge fund manager, thought that he could turn the company around. So, he acquired more than 50% of the outstanding shares. Consequently, the stock price went up 800%.

Joe Campbell couldn't sustain the losses from the stock soaring.

He initially started with about $30,000 in his brokerage account.

That was wiped out.

On top of that, he owed his brokerage over $100,000.

But he didn't have $100,000 in cash.

So, he had to liquidate his and his wife's 401ks and create a repayment plan with his brokerage.

Joe Campbell's life was ruined all because he overlooked an important risk. He thought that it was impossible for the stock to go up significantly. (After all, the company itself announced that it was shutting down). So, he shorted the stock. But, as he found out, the stock could go up quite a bit under certain circumstances. And he ended up taking on far more risk than he could bear the consequences of.

A main reason many investors overlook risk is that we are overconfident.

Here is a frequently cited statistic that illustrates this point. In the 1960s, a researcher surveyed two groups of motorists: one group of motorists who had just crashed their cars and another group of motorists who had "an excellent driving record." The motorists in each group were asked to rate their driving abilities on a scale from "expert" to "very poor."

You would expect the motorists who just had an accident to rate their driving abilities as poor. Conversely, you would expect the motorists with the excellent driving records to rate their driving abilities favorably.

But that's not what happened.

Motorists in each group, on average, rated their driving abilities at roughly the same level. In particular, both groups rated their driving abilities highly.

We like to think we are good at what we do—even if we clearly aren't.

The same concept applies to investing. We like to think we know more about a business than we really do. There is no better example of this than that of Coca-Cola. As mentioned in an earlier chapter, everyone likes to think that they understand Coca-Cola because it is an extraordinarily simple business. Yet, in reality, it's the business that most Wall Street professionals don't understand. They like to think they understand it. But they don't.

Similarly, when we overestimate our abilities, we think that we understand all of the risks, when we really don't. We end up like Joe Campbell. We think that the worst-case scenario isn't that bad, only to find our portfolio blown up because we missed a risk. Or, we end up like Ron Johnson. We think that we understand the potential impacts of our decision, only to realize that we severely underestimated the downside.

What's even worse is that conventional methods for identifying risks are almost certainly bound to fail.

Take the most common method of uncovering risks: researching the business. In order to uncover hidden risks, most investors thoroughly research the business and conduct "due diligence."

They read every earnings call.

They read the company's annual report.

They read the competition's annual report.

They read industry reports.

They read professional equity research reports.

They talk to management sometimes.

They talk to industry experts.

Yet, none of those methods can uncover hidden risks. Hidden risks are called 'hidden risks' for a reason. No one knows about them. Even after conducting significant due diligence, you are unlikely to come across them.

Joe Campbell, for example, could have done all the research he wanted to on KaloBios. He could have read their recent annual reports, and he could have read every news article about the company. But none of those information sources would have told him about the possibility of a turnaround. Heck, even the CEO of KaloBios didn't know that a turnaround was a possibility; the CEO announced themselves that they were seizing operations.

Instead, Joe Campbell was only able to learn about the hidden risk once it was too late—once the risk occurred.

Or consider Dexter Shoe from the previous chapter. Buffett could have spent hours talking to the management team at Dexter Shoe, but management didn't know anything about an impending offshore. Buffett could have spent all day reading industry reports on the domestic shoe industry, but none of them started to report on the offshoring risk until it occurred. He could have read equity research reports on other shoe manufacturers. But none of them would have indicated that Dexter Shoe would essentially collapse a few years after he bought into it.

Therefore, don't be the person who says, "It's important to conduct due diligence on an investment in order to understand all the risks associated with it." That's not true. You often can't understand the hidden risks of an investment better by reading more about the company.

If anything, having such a mindset will fool you. You'll say to yourself, "I've read every industry report, the company's annual report, and competitors' annual reports. I looked over the risk factors section in those documents, and I'm comfortable with all the risks listed. Therefore, I'll buy the stock." In the end, you'll end up learning that there were hidden risks—risks that can't be uncovered by merely reading reports and articles—and you'll end up taking on more risk than you can bear the consequences of.

Another method that investors use to uncover hidden risks is studying history.

Generally, studying history is an effective way to learn about many of the hidden risks in a business. At the very least, it is much more effective than reading current annual reports, current earnings transcripts, and current industry reports. When you only read current information, you are only exposed to one sample size of information. That one sample size is unlikely to contain all the major risks that can occur. On the other hand, if you immerse yourself in a decade's worth of history, you are more likely to come across all the potential risks that could occur.

However, studying history isn't perfect. History can only tell you about hidden risks that have occurred before. But many important hidden risks have not happened before.

Consider an instance in General Re, one of Berkshire Hathaway's property and casualty (P&C) reinsurance businesses.

For those who aren't familiar with insurance, a P&C insurance firm collects premiums (which are revenues for the P&C company) from customers. In return, the P&C insurance company becomes obligated to pay their customers claims (which is an expense for the P&C company) if the customer's property is damaged.

Before underwriting an insurance policy, a P&C insurer needs to estimate the potential claims that may arise from the policy so that they can estimate the profitability of an insurance policy. The insurance company always knows what the premiums (revenues) will be from taking on a new customer. That's written directly in their contract with the customer. What is unknown is the claims, which are determined by how much damage the property faces due to factors such as hail, hurricanes, and fires. Simply put, no one knows whether something like a hurricane or a fire will occur until they do occur. Moreover, no one knows how much damage they will cause. Hence, the insurance company must make an educated guess on how many claims will arise. Without estimating claims, they won't be able to determine whether underwriting an insurance policy is likely to be profitable (whether premiums are likely to exceed claims).

During the early 2000s, most insurers, including General Re, estimated claims mainly using historical data. For example, they looked at historical data on 1) how frequently natural disasters like hurricanes and tornados had occurred and 2) the damages they have caused. Then, they extrapolated those historical trends into the future to estimate what future claims might look like.

But relying solely on history was a mistake because an important hidden risk hadn't occurred before: major terrorist attacks.

On September 11th, 2001, the first terrorist attack of such scale occurred on the mainland of the USA, causing significant damages to several insured properties.

Since such an attack hadn't occurred on U.S. soil before, General Re never considered the possibility of it occurring when underwriting insurance. So, it never charged policyholders higher premiums ("prices") to compensate for the possibility of a terrorist attack. However, it was still responsible for paying $2.4 billion in claims to cover damages related to the attacks. In other words, it became responsible for paying terrorism-related claims ("expenses") without earning a premium ("revenue"). Hence, it grossly overestimated the risk-reward trade off, leading to one of the biggest insurance-underwriting mistakes of the time.

In Buffett's words:

> In pricing property coverages, for example, we had looked to the past and take into account only costs we might expect to incur from windstorm, fire, explosion and earthquake. But what will be the largest insured property loss in history (after adding related business-interruption claims) originated from none of these forces. In short, all of us in the industry made a fundamental underwriting mistake by focusing on experience, rather than exposure, thereby assuming a huge terrorism risk for which we received no premium.

Therefore, you can't expect to learn about every risk from studying history. Not every major risk that will occur in the future has occurred in the past. In the 1960s, people said, "Adidas will surely be the most dominant shoe company over the long term. After all, it had dominated every competitor for decades." Yet, in the 1970s, an unprecedented, hidden risk occurred: Nike. From there on out, it ceased to be the leader. In the early 2000s, people said, "MySpace will surely dominate over the long term. It has clearly been the market leader in its niche for several years." But a hidden risk would have proved them wrong: Facebook.

Therefore, you must be able to uncover all the important, hidden risks of an investment. It is never enough to assume that you can simply understand all the risks associated with an investment by merely reading current annual reports, current earnings transcripts, and current industry reports. That's the surest way to mis-assess risk. To truly be a safe investor, you must at least identify important, hidden risks before they actually occur, or else you'll end up blowing yourself up like Joe Campbell.

To help you with that, I'm going to provide you with a strategy called "Testing Your Assumptions."

TEST YOUR ASSUMPTIONS

Whenever you make a decision, there are always simple and basic assumptions embedded within that decision that make it a logical one.

To understand what I mean, let's consider a few non-investing examples. To start, consider whether the following statement is true.

Statement #1: "I made $2,500 last month after all expenses, including taxes. If I decide to buy a house and take on a mortgage payment of $2,000 per month, I will be able to afford it with $500 of wiggle room."

Do you think that statement is true or false?

In my view, it sounds perfectly logical. If you make $2,500 per month, and if you take on $2,000 in additional expenses, you will have $500 left over per month.[12]

However, that conclusion could also be totally wrong. It only holds true only if certain assumptions hold true. For example, in this scenario, the $2,500 figure was calculated using last month's income and expenses. In the future that figure might be different due to changes in the economy, changes in the job market, and the occurrence of random events (such as unexpected medical bills). Moreover, there were critical assumptions with the mortgage as well. For example, if it is a variable rate mortgage, the monthly payment might increase if interest rates increase, leaving you with less money. Therefore, the fact that $500 will be left over only holds true if a lot of other conditions hold true.

Let's say that an individual was in that scenario, trying to decide whether to take out a mortgage. If they don't think about

---

12   This example makes some big simplifications about the mechanics of mortgage payments.

the assumptions within their analysis, they will assume that they can afford the mortgage with $500 of wiggle room. On the other hand, if the same individual deeply considers those assumptions, they might realize that they can't afford the mortgage one bit. They might realize that their job isn't stable or that last month's expenses weren't predictive of future months' expenses, leading them to not take out a mortgage. In the end, it might prevent them from facing financial hardship.

Consider one more non-investing statement.

Statement #2: "During a final-round job interview, the candidate was told that he had the best interview yet. Therefore, the candidate concludes they will receive an offer from the company."

Is the conclusion of the scenario ("the candidate concludes they will receive an offer") logical or illogical?

On the surface, that conclusion sounds perfectly logical. After all, "if the interviewer says that the candidate was strong, surely they must get the job."

However, unless certain assumptions hold true, that conclusion can be totally wrong as well. What if a better candidate comes along in a later interview? In that case, the individual in the scenario wouldn't end up getting the job, assuming there is only one spot available. Or what if the needs of the employer change before the start date of the job? In that case, even though the candidate had the best interview, they still wouldn't end up with a job. Therefore, although the conclusion of statement #2 sounds perfectly logical, it can be totally wrong unless certain assumptions hold true.

Just as in the previous two scenarios the conclusions were logical but could have been totally wrong, your logical conclusions about investing can sound logical but be totally wrong if you overlook some critical assumptions.

In particular, if you fail to identify all the critical assumptions within your conclusions, you will overlook hidden risks.

There was once a manufacturer that was running a successful operation. Its product was known to have a strong brand within its industry. It had the largest market share among its competitors. Historically, sales growth for the business was in the mid-single digit ranges. It wasn't necessarily enticing to investors, but it was generally positive (with a few exceptions such as the 2008 recession).

But that started to change. After sales peaked a few years after the great recession, they started to slowly decline. At first, sales were declining by no more than just a couple of percentage points per quarter. As time went on, the decline started to accelerate, moving into the mid to high single digit range per quarter. When one compounds that decline over 30-40 quarters, those small numbers were making a big dent in the company's total sales.

After several years of not really doing much to address the declining sales and market share, management finally decided to take action. They increased the company's marketing budget, expecting that it would rejuvenate sales growth. So, they increased the marketing budget by 70% over 5 years—a very significant increase.

After hearing the company's investor relations presentation, Wall Street was happy because they saw that the marketing expenses were increasing. In a perfectly logical manner, they assumed that sales would grow as well. After all, the more money a company spends on marketing, the more people will know of the brand, and the more sales the company will produce. Consequently, the financial models of the stock analysts suddenly had higher revenue growth assumptions, and the stock price went up.

However, the marketing plan turned out to be a total disaster. Despite the 70% increase in marketing expenses, sales did not increase over the 5-year period. Generally, sales continued to decline at the exact same pace. After the failed 5-year marketing campaign, the company replaced the Vice President of Marketing.[13] The new Vice President of Marketing decided to cut the marketing

---

13   The company didn't have a Chief Marketing Officer, so the Vice President of Marketing was the highest marketing authority within the company. (I even reached out to him and offered help because his company kind of needed it).

budget to about its initial levels, and sales continued to decline at the same pace.

In the end, shareholders suffered because of the inability of management to prevent the sales declines. In fact, the stock had lost 40% of its market value over the 5-year period, and even to date, they still haven't fixed the problem of declining sales.

The interesting part about this manufacturing company is the contradictory relationship between the company's sales and marketing expenses. Like most investors, you would expect sales to increase significantly if more time and money are being devoted to marketing and selling the product. "After all, if a company spends more money on advertising its products, more people will know about it. If more people know about it, they make more money." But what really happened is that sales didn't move noticeably both when the company materially increased and decreased the marketing budget. Therefore, as exemplified by the manufacturing company, the conclusion that "materially increasing marketing expenses will lead to a material increase in sales" can sound perfectly logical but be totally wrong.

But why is that conclusion totally wrong?

Well, for a marketing effort to produce sales, a critical assumption must hold true: the marketing dollars have to be deployed effectively. Just as an investor could invest lots of money into businesses and not see a return if the companies fail, a company can invest a lot of money into marketing campaigns and not see a return if the marketing campaigns fail. In the case of the manufacturing company, that critical assumption clearly did not hold true. If it had, investors would have seen at least a little bit of sales growth over the 5-year period.

Thus, investors would have been far better off if they were conscious of that critical assumption. Certainly, they wouldn't have mindlessly increased their revenue projections for the company and assumed that growth is essentially guaranteed with more marketing spend. Instead, at the very least, they would have recognized that there was a very real, downside scenario where virtually no incremental revenue growth occurs. In other words, being aware of the assumptions within their conclusions would have made them aware of a hidden risk that the marketing campaigns would totally bomb—a risk that couldn't be easily identified by conducting research.

When investing, there are hundreds of different kinds of assumptions you can think about.

You think about assumptions related to a company's labor costs.

You think about assumptions related to a company's dividend and share repurchase policy.

You think about assumptions related to a company's recent acquisitions.

But the most important kinds of assumptions to think about are those related to a company's long-term competitive positioning.

Whenever you make any long-term investment, you are automatically assuming that the business will be competitive over the long term. Think about it. Under regular circumstances, it does not make sense to make a long-term investment unless you believe that the business will be competitive over the long term. After all, if you invest in a company that you think will see its competitive strength erode, you are essentially investing in a stock knowing that the business will weaken over time. That doesn't make too much sense. Therefore, the very act of making a long-term investment automatically implies that the investor believes the business will be competitive.[14]

It is important to make sure that that assumption—that the business will be competitive over the long term—is correct. If you don't think about that assumption very critically, you will likely end up investing in a business that will slowly see its competitive advantage deteriorate over time, leading to significant losses.

---

14   There is an exception to the argument of this paragraph. Sometimes, a weakening business can trade so cheaply that it makes sense to invest in it. But, in most cases, it doesn't make sense to invest in a business if you believe that the business will weaken over time.

Consider a personal example.

One time, for example, I was thinking about whether it made sense to invest in Netflix. I knew that understanding a company's long-term competitive strength is the core of successful investing, so I started with assessing its competitive advantage. As of the time I was doing this analysis, there was no question that Netflix was ahead of the competition. But the question I had to answer was whether it would be competitive over the long term. In a sense, I needed to know whether it was like one of the companies that were on Buffett's list of the top 20 largest companies in 1989; I needed to know whether it would continue to be dominant over the next 10 years or whether it would eventually end up losing its competitive edge.

I started to create a list of assumptions that needed to hold true for Netflix to be competitive over the long term. ("Netflix needs quality content." "Prices must be competitive." "Streaming has to be a competitive form of entertainment"). Then, I asked myself whether I could say, with a very high probability, that those assumptions would hold true. After thinking deeply about it, I realized that I couldn't be highly certain whether some of those assumptions would hold true. For example, I didn't feel as if I had concrete evidence to suggest that Netflix would have the highest quality content over the long term. It might, or it might not. I just wasn't sure. I didn't really know the second-layer drivers that could allow one company to have better or worse content. So, I didn't invest and moved on to something I felt more certain about.

Thinking through the assumptions helped me reach a more cautious conclusion about Netflix than most investors would have. Many people automatically assume that Netflix is an incredibly strong business because it is a "brand-name, FAANG stock." I would have come to the same conclusions myself if I didn't run through the assumptions. But I did, and it helped me realize that, frankly, Netflix wasn't within my circle of competence—just as

Charlie Munger would say that Apple isn't within his circle of competence.

There is one important thing to note, though. "Being aware of the conditions and assumptions that need to hold true for your conclusions to hold true" isn't simply an investment risk management strategy. It's a strategy for making accurate predictions in any area of life.

In his book *Think Again*, Adam Grant highlights the story of a forecaster: Jean-Pierre Beugoms. Jean-Pierre was a professional forecaster who competed in forecasting tournaments. In those tournaments, he competed against other forecasters in trying to predict world events like "who would win the next presidential election?" Or, as Adam Grant writes, "will an individual or a company face criminal charges for an accident involving a self-driving vehicle [next year]?"

But Jean-Pierre wasn't just any regular forecaster. He was an Outlier. As Adam Grant writes in *Think Again*:

> [Jean Pierre's] Brexit forecasts hovered in the 50 percent range when most of his competitors thought the referendum had little chance of passing. He successfully predicted that the incumbent would lose a presidential election in Senegal, even though the base rates of reelection were extremely high and other forecasters were expecting a decisive win. And he had, in fact, pegged Trump as the favorite long before pundits and pollsters even considered him a viable contender.

His strategy for making remarkable forecasts doesn't only involve researching the risks—the evidence that proves his predictions are potentially wrong. Instead, he also thinks critically about the conditions or assumptions that need to hold true for his conclusions to also hold true:

Jean-Pierre Beugoms has a favorite trick for catching himself when he's wrong. When he makes a forecast, he also makes a list of the conditions in which it should hold true—as well as the conditions under which he would change his mind. He explains that this keeps him honest, preventing him from getting attached to a bad prediction.

Don't only assess risk by conducting due diligence and research. That won't uncover hidden risks.

Instead, think critically about the assumptions embedded within your conclusions.

Known Unknowns

· ·

Many investors know that Warren Buffett invests in public companies. These are companies that anyone can buy stock in—companies like Apple and Walmart. You can simply open a brokerage account, search for AAPL and WMT, and buy their stocks.

But what not all investors—particularly new investors—are aware of is that Warren Buffett and Berkshire Hathaway can also invest in private companies. These are companies like SpaceX. If you open your Fidelity, Robinhood, or e-trade account and search "SpaceX" or "Aldi," they won't pop up. That's because these companies are not available to the public to invest in (at least as of today). Instead, only certain types of entities—Berkshire Hathaway, private equity firms, large corporations, rich individuals—can invest in them.

Typically, private equity firms—investment firms that typically invest in private businesses—are highly involved with their investments.

When you invest in a public company like Apple, you cannot get involved in its operations. You cannot tell Apple which products to launch, which marketing campaigns to run, and which banks to borrow money from.

Private equity is often the opposite. They often can and will get very involved in a company's operations. For example, they commonly invest in companies and then decide to fire people to save labor costs. One study, for example, found that employment in private equity backed companies decreases by 5%, on average, after they make an investment.

Other times, they may dictate the growth strategy of a company. I remember that when I was a freshman in college, a very friendly individual named Asad Abdullah gave me an internship at his private equity firm, Radazon Capital. While there, I did a lot of work—which was hopefully helpful—to dictate the growth strategy of our holding companies. I brainstormed different markets that they could expand into, and I forecasted how much revenue they could make if they successfully penetrated those markets. I even made a PowerPoint on how a holding company could improve its website user interface to, ideally, increase conversions.

It is perfectly logical for private equity firms to get involved in a company's operations. Why wouldn't they? It helps them make money. Private equity firms are often able to identify strategies to grow sales and reduce expenses in the companies they invest in. Assuming those strategies are good, they can increase the profitability of their businesses, ultimately increasing their own return on investment.

But what's interesting is that Warren Buffett has a totally different approach.

When Buffett buys private companies, he rarely gets involved in their operations at all. Generally speaking, he does not tell the CEOs of his own companies how to position their product, what marketing campaigns to run, or what profit margins they need to hit. In a previous annual meeting, for example, Buffett stated that he doesn't have the CEOs and Chief Financial Officers of his private companies send him budgets. Even though Berkshire Hathaway often owns the majority or entirety of those businesses, Buffett doesn't require them to tell him how much they plan on spending. In some cases, he doesn't even talk to them at all:

> The CEO of one of our most successful subsidiaries, I may have talked to—unless I saw him here [at the Berkshire Hathaway annual meeting] and just said

> hello—I've probably talked to him three times in
> the last 10 years. And he does remarkably well. He
> might have done even better if I hadn't talked to
> him those three times.

Based on my research, there are two main reasons why Buffett, unlike most private equity firms, doesn't get involved in the operations of his holding companies.

The first is simply that it helps attract high-quality talent. People like autonomy. People don't like having a boss who micromanages. So, Buffett provides autonomy to the CEOs that work for him by not getting involved in their operations. That effectively makes Berkshire Hathaway a much more desirable place for CEOs to work, allowing Buffett to attract talent away from many private equity firms.

The second reason—which is more important for the purposes of this chapter—is that Buffett knows far less about his own businesses than the CEOs that run them.

Just think about it.

As we will discuss in detail later, Buffett often makes acquisition decisions very quickly. In fact, he can sometimes make the decision within just a few hours of hearing about the company. In 2001, the owner of a picture frame company, Larson-Juhl, wanted to sell his business to Buffett and contacted him. They talked on the phone for 15 minutes. During that call, Buffett concluded that it was potentially a good investment—even though he had never heard of the company previously. So, he invited the business owner into his office in Omaha, Nebraska, and they discussed the business a little more. At the office, Buffett questioned the business owner for just 90 minutes, when he decided to officially invest in the company. Therefore, in just 105 minutes, Buffett acquired the entire company.

In 105 minutes, you can learn a lot about a company. In Buffett's case, he learned enough to invest in it.

But in just 105 minutes, he wasn't going to learn everything. He learned a lot, but not nearly as much as the business owner who had been running it for 20 years. Therefore, Buffett isn't as capable of making operating decisions as the business owner who has decades of experience running the actual business. In Buffett's own words, it would be the "height of foolishness" for him to tell his CEOs how to run their companies.

Buffett generally has a similar approach to public companies as well. Although he has read every single Coca-Cola annual report published since 1988, he doesn't tell Coca-Cola's Chief Marketing Officer how to improve Coca-Cola's brand.[15] He doesn't know more about marketing, sales, and branding than Coca-Cola's Chief Marketing Officer. Although Buffett has read every single Bank of America annual report from the last 50+ years, he doesn't tell the CEO how to grow deposits and how to calculate what interest rate to charge. He doesn't know more about running a bank than the CEO of an actual bank.

The fact that Warren Buffett doesn't get involved in his businesses illustrates an important lesson for all investors: you can study a business incredibly closely, but still be far away from understanding everything about it. That was the case with Coca-Cola and Bank of America. Although Warren Buffett has studied those companies more closely than nearly every investor alive, he knows that there is still a lot that he doesn't know about them.

In fact, you often won't know everything that's important to making an investment decision in a company.

Let's say that you are thinking about investing in Disney. As a part of your research process, you would want to build your second layer of competence around Disney. To do so, you would not only need to recognize that Disney has phenomenal content that creates a great customer experience (the first layer of competence), but also, in theory, you would need to understand what could strengthen or weaken Disney's content. The second layer of

---

15   A counter argument to this point would be that Warren Buffett sat on Coca-Cola's board of directors, where he may have advised the management team. But even as a board member, Buffett's involvement wouldn't have been nearly as deep as that of many private equity firms.

competence around content would allow you to thoroughly assess whether anything could diminish Disney's ability to deliver a superior customer experience in the future.

However, it is unrealistic to expect that you could build a second layer of competence around Disney's content quality and customer experience. It's simply not that easy. You can build a second layer of competence around Disney's brand. You can find lots of books, articles, and studies on what causes brands to succeed and fail. But the same can't be said for Disney's content quality. You could probably spend hours and hours reading about what makes great content. But you're unlikely to come across the important, second-layer drivers that make Disney's content better than everyone else's. If anything, that information is kept secret by key Disney personnel because they don't want people copying what they are doing.

Does that mean you can't invest in Disney? Is the fact that you don't have a second layer of competence around Disney's content quality a big enough reason to conclude that you don't understand Disney? Well, no.

You can't avoid investing in a company merely because you don't have your second layer circle of competence fully developed.

The reality is that you don't have your second layer of competence fully developed on almost any company.

Take Mars-Wrigley, the company that owns Skittles, M&M's, and Snickers, as an example. To truly understand everything about its competitiveness, you would need to understand how difficult it would be to create a better-tasting candy. That requires a basic understanding of food science. But I doubt you know anything about food science.

Or take Fruit of the Loom as an example. To truly understand how difficult it would be to overthrow Fruit of the Loom, you would want to understand how difficult it would be to create underwear that consumers like better than Fruit of the Loom's. But you can't understand that. You would need a deep understanding of product development and how consumers evaluate underwear. That's not feasible for everyone to understand.

Outlier Investors recognize that they rarely understand everything about a business, but they ensure that they know just enough to make an intelligent investment decision. In fact, that's exactly what Warren Buffett does. As mentioned earlier, he doesn't know everything about his privately owned companies. That's why he doesn't tell his CEOs what to do. Yet, at the same time, he feels that he knows enough to invest in them in the first place. Similarly, Warren Buffett doesn't know every little detail about Coca-Cola and Bank of America, even though he has read dozens of their annual reports. But he knows that he knows enough to make an investment in both of those companies.

In fact, being able to know when you know enough and when you don't know enough is critical to making investment decisions.

If you underestimate how much you know, you'll end up passing on great opportunities. Some of Berkshire Hathaway's major mistakes occurred because Warren Buffett and Charlie Munger underestimated what they knew. For example, they were analyzing Google in its early days. They concluded that it was a terrific business. Moreover, they thought they had a reasonable understanding of its economics. However, they were still hesitant to pull the trigger. They weren't entirely sure whether they understood it because it was a technology company, a type of company that they found hard to understand. So, they decided to not invest in it. In hindsight, of course, we know that Buffett and Munger really did know that Google was a terrific company, but they were simply underestimating how much they knew. As Munger recounted in a Berkshire Hathaway annual meeting:

> I feel like a horse's [expletive] for not identifying Google better... We screwed up... We could see in our own operations how well Google advertising was working. And we just sat there sucking our thumbs.

Conversely, overestimating how much you understand can ruin your life. In fact, that's exactly what happened to Joe Campbell in an earlier chapter. He was likely certain that KaloBios couldn't go up because the company was liquidating. So, he made a significant short position in the security. However, he quickly learned that he didn't understand all the major risks associated with the investment, such as the risk that someone attempts to turn the company around. As a result, he blew away his life savings.

To help you know when you know enough and when you don't, I'm going to share two tools with you. The first is called Stress Testing, which will help you make decisions when your second layer of competence isn't fully developed. The second tool is called the Important Knowns matrix. The Important Knowns Matrix is a decision-making tool that can help you systematically figure out whether you know enough about a business to make an intelligent investment decision.

STRESS TESTING

· ·

I decided not to tell you an important piece of information in an earlier chapter.

In the chapter called Follow The 80% Past Rule, we talked about how the world's most successful investors are obsessed with studying history. Warren Buffett read more than 10 years' worth of Coca-Cola annual reports before investing in the company. Ray Dalio realized that one of his biggest early career mistakes came from not studying history closely. And Charlie Munger read nearly every single General Motors annual report to learn about its history.

We also talked about the types of annual reports that you should focus on reading, such as the reports of a company's early history and the reports of companies that have failed.

But there was one type of annual report that I didn't tell you about. Frankly, it's one of the most important ones.

What type of annual report it is? The annual report that allows you to stress test a business against certain risks.

After the 2008 financial crisis, the federal authorities made changes to how they regulated banks. One of these changes implemented strict stress testing requirements.

Stress tests test a bank's resiliency to various risk factors. When stress testing, a bank runs a simulation to see whether they will make it through any major crises that could impact it. For example, the risk management team will ask themselves, "if housing prices fall 20%, will we have enough assets to meet our liabilities? If the unemployment rate increases by 4% tomorrow and the economy slows down, will we be able to stay solvent? If unemployment rises and the economy tanks, will we have enough capital to withstand the crisis?"

Just as a bank stress tests itself to understand its resiliency to certain risk factors, you can stress test your business. Of course, the average investor can't use a fancy model like banks to stress test a business. But what can be used is history.

Whenever you are unsure of the second-layer drivers of a business, what you can do is stress test it. To do so correctly, you want to identify what you don't fully understand about a source of a company's competitive advantage. Is it its product quality? Its ability to produce goods at a lower cost? Or something else? Then, you want to look back at history at times when that competitive advantage was under attack. That will give you a sense of the company's resiliency to certain competitive threats.

For example, one time I was thinking about Disney's competitive strength.

I knew that it was a highly competitive business. For one, Disney has an incredibly strong brand. When people are thinking about where to go for a vacation, the Disney parks are almost always at the top of their minds. In fact, its brand is so strong that it attracts more visitors than Hawaii. According to one source, about 20 million people visit the Disney parks every year, while only 10 million people visit Hawaii every year. Moreover, I knew that Disney had very entertaining content. Over the decades, viewers have built a habit of watching Disney merely because it has consistently pushed out high quality content. Children could binge watch the Disney channel day in and day out, but the same couldn't be said about many other programs.

However, I was hesitant to conclude that I understood it because there was a known unknown: something that you know you don't know. I knew that I didn't understand the second-layer drivers of what makes good content. I didn't know the likelihood that a company would be able to create more entertaining content. Did Disney have a secret sauce that made it very difficult for competitors to create better content? Or could people just reverse engineer their content because it was widely available? Moreover, I didn't know what the consequences were of someone creating higher quality content. Would Disney slowly start to lose its viewers? Would it rapidly decline? Or would it continue to grow? I personally didn't know.

So, I stress tested the business. I looked back at history at times when competitors created high quality content and other forms of entertainment. I looked back at the time when YouTube started gaining traction to see whether Disney started to decline. I looked back at the time when Netflix started to see whether Disney was resilient. And I looked back at the time when famous YouTubers started their YouTube channels and perhaps distributed more addictive content than Disney to see whether people stopped watching Disney.

What I found was very interesting. Even though Disney has faced many headwinds over the past two decades—declines in TV viewership, the rise of Netflix, the growth of gaming, the creation of YouTube—people continued to watch Disney's content. From 2000 to 2020, Disney's media networks' revenue—sales Disney earns from distributing its content through platforms like cable, satellite, and Hulu—have generally grown.[16] Similarly, Disney's media networks'

---

16   Media network revenues don't include revenue from Disney's parks and streaming platform. Therefore, it is a better proxy of Disney's non-streaming viewership than total revenue.

operating income has consistently grown from 2000 to 2020, even though the business has faced significant threats to its competitive advantage over that period.

Disney's sales climbed from 2000-2020, despite significant threats to its competitive positioning

Disney's Media Networks revenue and operating income ($ in millions) from 2000 to 2022

Source: Capital IQ

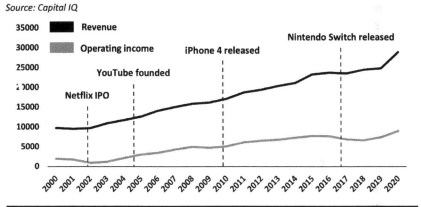

What that told me is that Disney's business is incredibly resilient to competitive threats. Netflix can come out with great shows. But Disney could fight through. The number of cable subscribers can decline substantially. But Disney can still manage to grow sales. YouTube could produce, perhaps, more addictive content than Disney. iPhone's app store, Sony's PlayStation, and Microsoft's Xbox could come out with incredibly entertaining games, but Disney could still manage to pull through.

So, even though I didn't understand the second-layer drivers of why people entertain themselves one way or another, I was able to understand that the risk of someone creating superior content was low. I had a lot of data to prove it. No matter what sorts of competitive threats Disney has faced—the rise of mobile gaming, the Xbox,

Netflix, or Hulu—it has managed to continually entertain individuals as well as the competition. It could face enormous stressors, but still pull through.

Therefore, whenever you don't understand the second-layer drivers of a business, stress test it.

If you don't understand the risk of someone coming out with a better product, stress test it. Look at times in history when a competitor came out with a better product and understand how the business reacted. Was it resilient? Or did the company's competitive advantage erode?

If you don't understand how a natural disaster could impact an insurance company, stress test it. Look at times in history when major natural disasters occurred. What kind of balance sheet did it need to survive such an event? Does it have that kind of balance sheet today?

However, it is important to note that stress testing should never be used as a replacement for building your second layer of competence.

Stress testing is only effective to the extent that the business has faced significant stressors before. If many companies hadn't attempted to create a better customer experience than Disney, I wouldn't have been able to stress test Disney. There simply wouldn't have been history that could help me understand how Disney would fare if competitors attempted to create a better customer experience. Similarly, stress testing an insurance company wouldn't be accurate if future risks are larger than historical risks. If a magnitude 7.0 earthquake is the worst risk an insurer has faced historically, stress testing won't be useful if a magnitude 9.5 earthquake and a pandemic occur tomorrow. An insurance company would need a much larger balance sheet to survive both a 9.5 magnitude earthquake and a pandemic than simply one 7.0 magnitude earthquake. But history wouldn't be able to tell you what kind of balance sheet an insurer would need to survive a 9.5 magnitude earthquake during a pandemic simply because that kind of risk hadn't occurred before. Therefore, you wouldn't be able to evaluate whether the insurance company would make it through the unprecedented 9.5 magnitude earthquake and pandemic.

In fact, it is not uncommon for unprecedented levels of risk to occur. As Nassim Taleb once wrote in a *Harvard Business Review* article:

> Risk managers mistakenly use hindsight as foresight. Alas, our research shows that past events don't bear any relation to future shocks. World War I, the attacks of September 11, 2001—major events like those didn't have predecessors. The same is true of price changes. Until the late 1980s, the worst decline in stock prices in a single day had been around 10%. Yet prices tumbled by 23% on October 19, 1987. Why then would anyone have expected a meltdown after that to be only as little as 23%? History fools many.

One time, in fact, I was having trouble stress testing a business because the business hadn't faced as high levels of risks in the past. I was analyzing a specialty retailer that was trading at 3.5x earnings. Although it didn't have a large competitive advantage in the brick-and-mortar space, it was a decent business. From a financial standpoint, it was producing higher sales per square foot than most retailers, and it was producing good returns on capital.

But there was a reason that the stock was trading so low. The industry was being disrupted. One of the company's competitors was launching an incredibly strong omnichannel distribution strategy. In fact, the competitor had pulled all their merchandise off Amazon because they knew that they could more effectively reach consumers using their own website and app. Moreover, everyone knew that the company I was analyzing wouldn't be able to create as competitive of a business strategy as the competition. The competition simply had a huge edge over the company I was analyzing.

Personally, I didn't fully understand all the important second-layer drivers of the business. So, I didn't understand the degree to which the competition would diminish the company's long-term cash-generating ability. That made it difficult to determine whether the business was overvalued or undervalued at a P/E ratio of 3.5.

Moreover, it was difficult to stress test the business. The long-term prospects of the business had never been threatened to that degree. So, I couldn't go back to history to see what had happened when the business faced similar risks. There was simply no history to go to.

As a result, I had to pass on the company. It was tempting to invest in the decent company since its P/E ratio was only 3.5. But I didn't understand the risks involved in the investment, nor did I understand what the business would look like over the long term. So, I had to remain disciplined and move on to analyzing another company.

Had I really understood the second-layer drivers of the business, however, I would have been able to predict its future. When you truly understand the second-layer drivers of a business, you don't need stress testing. Remember Nick Sleep? He was the investor who bought Amazon in the early 2000s. He didn't need to stress test competitors to predict Amazon's success. Even if he had wanted to, he wouldn't have been able to. Amazon was an unprecedented event, so there was no history. Yet, he was still able to understand that Amazon would be successful because he had a thorough understanding of its second-layer drivers.

Therefore, always prioritize building a second layer of competence. That is always the best way to understand a business and predict its future. However, you won't always understand all the second-layer drivers of a business. That's where stress testing comes in. It allows you to develop some level of understanding about the things you don't currently understand. In a sense, it allows you to close any remaining gaps in your understanding.

Although it is inferior to developing a second layer of competence, it is a great backup for when you can't fully develop a second layer of competence on a business.

THE IMPORTANT KNOWNS MATRIX

In the 1998 Berkshire Hathaway annual meeting, an investor asked Warren Buffett two big questions about the prospects of the economy:

1. What is your view on the global "financial business environment [over] the next decade?"

2. What is your view on the "U.S. position for economic competition in the next decade?"

In response, Buffett said something that may have stunned some people:

> You've asked two big questions, but you're going to get very small answers... We don't think about those things very much... Our views in the past wouldn't have been any good on those subjects... [Instead], we try to think about two things. We try to think about things that are important and things that are knowable.

That last sentence captures an important point about good decision-making. Always focus on what's knowable and what's important.

Every piece of information can be classified as either being important or unimportant and knowable or unknowable. Think of it like a 2 by 2 matrix. Any piece of information will fall within one of the four quadrants.

The Important Knowns Matrix

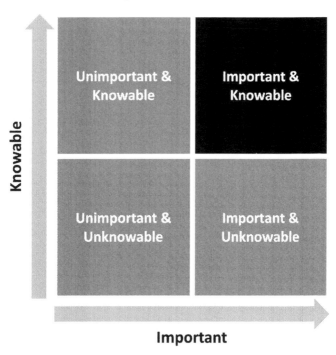

Important pieces of information are critical to predicting a company's long-term success. These are pieces of information that you should obsess about understanding. Some examples of important pieces of information are brand strength, product quality, management quality, company culture, and cost-efficiency. Those factors are the 20% of drivers that determine 80% of a company's long-term success. Hence, investors should research them deeply.

On the other hand, unimportant pieces of information are those that aren't useful for predicting a company's long-term success. Some examples are GDP growth rates, inflation rates, foreign exchange rates, market cycles, presidential elections, (some) industry trends, investment styles, (some) short-term headwinds, (some) short-term tailwinds, temporary company issues, dividend yields, most share repurchase policies, stock price targets, expected multiple compression, and many more things. Those factors simply don't tell you whether a business will succeed over the long term. If you were going to bet on whether Walmart would be more or less successful in five years, I don't think factors like inflation rates, market cycles, share repurchase policies, and dividend yields would be the focus of your analysis. So, they shouldn't be the focus of your research. Even if the media and other investors are focusing on them, long-term investors shouldn't.

Knowable pieces of information are those that you can understand by conducting thorough research. The quality of Disney's customer experience was a factor that was, within reason, knowable to me. I was able to stress test Disney to better understand the competitive risks regarding its content quality. A company's cost-efficiency can be knowable if you analyze its profit margins. Consumer behavior can be understandable if you read books and articles about why businesses succeed and fail. Therefore, knowable pieces of information are those that you can understand if you conduct research. And they should be researched if they are important.

On the other hand, unknowable pieces of information are those that you can't understand. Some examples of unknowable pieces of information are: what will the regulatory environment look like in three years? What P/E ratio will a company trade at in two years? Will there be a recession this year? How does the company allocate their R&D budget? In many cases, no matter how much research you do, you won't be able to understand those pieces of information. Essentially, no one knows for certain whether there will be a recession two years from now, and most companies won't break down their cost structure on a granular level.

When investing, you should not spend time trying to learn things that are unknowable. That's simply a waste of time. You'll spend hours and hours studying them, but they won't help you make a sound investment decision. To some people, for example, knowing what P/E ratio a company will trade at next year might be important. According to them, it impacts the future price of a company's stock. However, it wouldn't be intelligent to consider what a company's future P/E ratio will be when making an investment decision. That is an unknowable figure; unless you know what investors' opinions of the company will be next year, you can't know what a company's future P/E ratio will be. If you based an investment decision on what you think the P/E ratio will be, you would be basing it on an assumption that you aren't sure holds true. But, as mentioned in the "Test Your Assumptions" section of the "Find Hidden Risks" chapter, relying on unknown assumptions is a sure way to make a poor decision. Therefore, you'll make a poor investment if you focus on analyzing factors that are simply unknowable.

I created a list of three questions based on the Important Knowns Matrix. Asking yourself these three questions before making any investment decision will help you decide whether you know enough about a business to come to an intelligent investment decision.

QUESTION #1:
ARE THERE ANY PIECES OF INFORMATION THAT ARE BOTH UNKNOWABLE AND IMPORTANT?

The first question to ask yourself is whether there are any pieces of information that are important but unknowable.

If no pieces of information fall into this category, that's great. That means that all the important factors about the business are understandable with some research.

If a couple of pieces of information fall in this category, it's not the end of the world.

In fact, it's not uncommon for important things to be unknowable. For example, an important determinant of a CEO's quality is their business philosophy. How do they make business decisions?

How innovative are they? How much do they obsess over making customers happy? Although it is important to be able to answer those questions to assess a CEO's quality, you often won't be able to do so. Annual reports don't always provide much insight into that. Moreover, the average investor can't call a manager and ask them about their business philosophy.

There is a simple tactic for handling factors that are important yet unknowable.

What you want to do is create a list of every piece of information that's unknowable and important. Then, you want to go through your list and ask yourself, "am I comfortable investing in the business if I don't know this important factor?"

In some cases, the answer might be "yes." A company's product might be so strong that you are comfortable not knowing the CEO's business philosophy, for example. If so, feel free to invest in the company.

In other cases, however, the answer might be "no." That's what happened to me with the specialty retailer that was trading at 3.5x earnings. In that case, there was an important factor that I didn't know about: the strength of the company's long-term competitive positioning. So, I asked myself, "would I be comfortable owning the business knowing that I don't understand its long-term competitive positioning?" And I concluded that I wouldn't. Therefore, I didn't invest in the security because I didn't have enough knowledge to make an intelligent investment decision.

QUESTION #2:
AM I BASING AN INVESTMENT DECISION ON ANYTHING THAT'S KNOWABLE AND UNIMPORTANT?

The second question you want to ask yourself is, "Am I basing my investment decision on anything that's knowable but unimportant to a company's long-term success?"

If the answer is "no," that's great. You don't want to base your investment decisions on factors that don't matter over the long term.

If you find that you are basing investment decisions on factors that don't matter, stop. Forget about those unimportant pieces of information. As an investor, you must always focus on the 20% of factors that produce 80% of results. So, it would be unintelligent to base any long-term investment decision on something that you know is unimportant to a company's long-term success.

The big danger associated with even considering unimportant pieces of information is that they can bias your thinking.

In some cases, they can cause you to falsely believe that an investment is far better than it really is. I'll share an example that we'll look at more extensively in a future chapter: that of Blockbuster.

At the time, many investors were bullish on Blockbuster. Blockbuster had a strong brand. It was the dominant service in its niche. The CEO saw several ways to increase margins quickly. Blockbuster's market penetration wasn't high, so there were opportunities to increase market share.

But, at the end of the day, all those reasons were insignificant to the fact that Netflix developed a better product. Of course, Blockbuster's brand was not unimportant. However, there is no question that it was unimportant when compared to the importance of having a great product. Of course, having several ways to grow margins by a couple of percentage points isn't totally unimportant. But it was peanuts relative to the importance of having a competitive product. And of course, focusing on growth opportunities is not unimportant. But it was completely insignificant relative to the importance of having a great product.

In a sense, investors who were bullish on Blockbuster had biased thinking by focusing on relatively unimportant factors. They focused on all the factors that were unimportant relative to product quality: slight margin expansion, the large market size, and Blockbuster's strong brand. Consequently, they thought that Blockbuster would succeed. After all, their minds were filled with lots of reasons why Blockbuster would succeed. However, those reasons were relatively unimportant when compared to product quality, which they didn't think deeply about. As a result, investors' predictions of Blockbuster's success were off.

In other cases, focusing on unimportant information that's knowable can cause you to be overly pessimistic about a stock, causing you to miss out on big investment opportunities. Take Coca-Cola as an example.

Coca-Cola had lots of problems when it went public in 1919. Coca-Cola had "conflict[s] with the sugar industry and its bottlers," which caused the stock to go from $40 per share to $19 per share.

Many people would have been fearful of investing in Coca-Cola at the time. "I don't want to invest in a company that's having many legitimate business problems that caused it to lose over 50% of its market value."

But the reality is that all those problems were unimportant in the long-term—even though they caused the company to lose over 50% of its market value in the short term. What was far more important to know was that they would eventually build one of the strongest brands in the world and that they would be able to make customers happy. As Warren Buffett once recounted:

> Coca-Cola went public in—I think it was—1919.
> And the first year, one share cost $40. The first
> year, it went down to a little over 50%. At the end
> of the year, it went down to $19. There were some
> problems with bottler contracts. There was some
> problem with sugar, and [there were] various other
> kinds of problems... But the important thing wasn't
> to see that. The important thing was to see that they
> were going to be selling a billion 8-ounce servings
> of beverages a day... and that the person who could
> make people happy a billion times a day around the
> globe ought to make a few bucks off doing it. So
> that $40, which went down to $19, I think—with
> dividends reinvested—has to be well over $5 million

now. And if you developed a view on these other subjects that in any way forestalled you acting on this more specific, narrow view about the future of the company, you would have missed a great ride.

QUESTION #3:
DO I THINK I KNOW EVERYTHING THAT'S KNOWABLE AND IMPORTANT?

I know of an investor who was planning to invest in a consumer products business. He thought, "this consumer products company is phenomenal. Brands are important for consumer goods, and this company's brand is strong. Everyone knows about this company's brand. It's the number one brand in its category, and the company's competitors don't even have a brand that's nearly as strong at all. The company is even extremely cheap. Its P/E ratio is only 9. That's a steal."

He bought the company that same day.

Wondering whether it was actually a good investment opportunity, I looked up the company on Statista, a company that aggregates market data. I saw a report that compared its brand strength metrics relative to its competitors. What I found contradicted everything that that investor said. The company's brand awareness was not stronger than its competitors at all. The company had very little brand awareness. I had never heard of the company, and most people in America, according to the data, hadn't either.

I had no idea what kind of research that guy did. But I can tell you that it wasn't thorough at all.

Don't think that you are any different from that guy. We are all guilty of not thoroughly researching a stock before buying it.

To predict which companies will succeed and fail, you must study which companies have succeeded and failed in the past. But I will guarantee you that very few people have read the reports of companies that have failed. People say, "I'm incredibly confident that this restaurant will succeed over the long-term." Yet, you can ask them, "have you read the annual report of the restaurant that went out of business last year?" And they'll say, "no, I've only read the annual report of the restaurant that I'm planning on investing in." Yet, they expect to understand whether their restaurant passes the Billion Dollar Test and whether it will fail.

Or they say, "I may not understand semiconductor companies, the latest startup, or biotech stocks. But I understand brands, so I stick to investing in good brands." Then you ask them, "Do you know what makes Coca-Cola's brand stronger than Pepsi's or McDonald's brand better than Burger King's?" In response, they say, "I don't know, but I know I understand brands."

You must realize that you don't understand everything that's knowable and important unless you do thorough research. You shouldn't expect to know everything that's knowable and important without at least reading outdated annual reports. You shouldn't expect to understand simple topics like branding and consumer behavior if you've simply never studied them. I'm serious. As illustrated earlier, everyone thinks that they understand businesses like Coca-Cola—even without doing any research into the business.

Before you buy any stock, you want to be able to say, "I've researched this business so well that there is essentially nothing else that I could learn that's both knowable and important. I could pick up most books, annual reports, and articles on the business and industry and confidently tell myself 'I doubt I'll find any important pieces of information that I don't already know.' On top of that, everything that I could want to know about the business—when the CEO will pass away, what its exact profit margins will be next quarter, whether the company will be involved in WW III—is completely unknowable, making it a poor use of time for me to continue researching the business."

Simply put, if you don't understand everything that's knowable and important, you haven't finished doing your research yet. Knowing that there is important and knowable information that you haven't read yet means that you are ignoring pieces of information that could completely change your view of a company's prospects.

As Warren Buffett told the individual who asked the "two big questions" about the macroeconomy:

> We try to think about things that are important and things that are knowable. Now, there are things that are important that are not knowable. In our view, those two questions that you raised fall in that. There are things that are knowable but not important. We don't want to clutter our minds up with those... We say, 'what is important and what is knowable.' And, what among the things that fall into those two categories can we translate into some kind of an action.

The Important Knowns Matrix

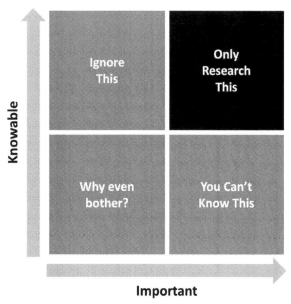

Average investors focus on knowable things that are unimportant and important things that are unknowable, while Outliers only focus on what's knowable and important.

What's important is what impacts a company's long-term cash-generating ability—and nothing else. In 1919, Coca-Cola stock fell from $40 to $19 due to very real bottler and sugar problems. But you would have missed out on that $19 turning into $5,000,000 if you concluded that those problems were important.

THINK LIKE AN OUTLIER

Invest on First Principles

Back in 1972, Warren Buffett and Charlie Munger met with an entrepreneur who had started her business when she was 70 years old, and they were interested in acquiring it.

The business had a phenomenal competitive advantage in the market. In particular, it had a strong brand that everyone loved. In fact, one time, a later CEO of the business attempted to stop selling 14 of the company's products to keep the product line at about 100 items. What was the response by the customers? Were they agnostic? By all means they weren't. Since customers loved the products so much, they flooded the company with letters saying that the company must continue selling those products. The customers simply couldn't live without the company's products.

Despite the company's strong competitive advantage and high quality, Buffett and Munger were hesitant about buying the business.

It just looked a little too expensive.

At the time, Buffett practiced what was known as a cigar-butt investment strategy—a strategy that he had learned from Ben Graham. The essence of that strategy was to buy very cheap stocks. He ideally wanted the business to be so cheap that it cost less than its net tangible assets (i.e. below liquidation value). For example, on a very simple level, if a business had $1 million in cash, assuming that cash was the company's only asset and that it had no debt, Buffett would have wanted to pay less than $1 million for the business.

The business that Buffett and Munger were thinking about buying in 1972 wasn't nearly that cheap. It had cost roughly $25 million to buy, and it had $8 million in net tangible assets. In an ideal world, they would have wanted to pay less than $8 million for the business since it had $8 million in net tangible assets. However, since the business owner was asking $25 million for it, they thought that the business cost too much to buy. Despite its high price, however, they didn't want to reject the deal right away due to the company's high quality and profitability.

Unsure of whether to make the investment, Munger decided to ask his friend Ira Marshall, a petroleum engineer, what he thought they should do. Marshall told Munger—in a blunt manner—to buy the business:

> You guys are all wrong on this. This is a wonderful company, and you're being way too chancy. There aren't many companies like this. There are some things you should pay up for... You're underestimating quality.

After hearing Marshall's advice, Munger and Buffett "listened to [his] criticism." They thought that perhaps Marshall was right and that they were wrong. So, they "changed [their] minds." They decided to buy the company at a premium compared to what they had ideally wanted to pay for it.

This company—See's Candies—turned out to be one of the most successful investments made by Berkshire Hathaway. According to Business Insider, See's Candies has returned over 8000% since it was purchased back in 1972. In fact, Buffett even said during a 2019 Berkshire Hathaway shareholder meeting that:

> We put $25 million into it and it's given us over $2 billion of pretax income, well over $2 billion.

What were even more important than the monetary gains were the lessons that they learned from See's Candies. After seeing that See's Candies turned out to be a successful investment, even though they paid slightly more money for it, they learned that it can be good idea to pay a premium for higher quality businesses. After that, Buffett started to shift his investment strategy to focus on buying high quality businesses at fair prices (such as See's Candies) rather than buying low quality businesses at low prices—such as buying a business that has $1 million in cash for less than $1 million. Ultimately, this lesson led Buffett to invest in Coca-Cola, which has turned out quite well. According to Berkshire Hathaway's most recent annual report, Coca-Cola was purchased for about $1.299 billion. As of the most recent annual filing, that investment is worth $23.684 billion, producing incredible gains for Berkshire Hathaway.

The lesson that many people take away from this story is that it can be a good idea to pay up a little for a business if you are getting quality. That is, on the surface, what the story line is after all. Buffett and Munger weren't thinking about investing in See's Candies. Someone came along and told them about the importance of considering business quality. The pair of investors changed their mind, and it turned out to be a success.

However, there is a much deeper lesson about critical thinking within the story. That is, perfectly logical ideas can be terribly wrong.

Put yourself in Buffett's and Munger's shoes before they sought advice from Ira Marshall. At the time, Buffett's investment strategy was to ideally buy a company for $1 that could be liquidated for more than $1. That's how he had been making money for most of his investment career at the time. That's even what Ben Graham taught him to do.

So, when Buffett saw that See's Candies couldn't be purchased below liquidation value, would it have been illogical to avoid investing in See's Candies? Absolutely not. It would have sounded perfectly logical to Buffett to avoid buying See's Candies.

For one, you make money by investing in undervalued businesses—businesses that are cheap. Therefore, it would have sounded logical to be hesitant about buying a company like See's Candies, which wasn't very cheap.

Secondly, Buffett's investment history would have made him think that buying See's Candies would have been illogical. Since Buffett had a track record of making large returns when he bought businesses that were trading significantly below their liquidation value, and a track record of not making as much money when he bought businesses at a premium to liquidation value, he learned that it is a good idea to avoid businesses that are trading at a premium to liquidation value. Therefore, it would have sounded perfectly logical in his mind to not buy See's Candies.

The problem is that his perfectly logical conclusions were entirely wrong. In hindsight, it was a phenomenal idea to invest in See's Candies. Who would argue that earning over 8000% returns is a bad idea? Who wouldn't want to pay $25 million for a business that would earn over $2 billion in pretax profits?

What this illustrates is that you can have ideas that sound perfectly logical but are entirely wrong.

Not being able to identify and get rid of perfectly logical yet terrible illogical ideas is a major source of investment failure. We almost saw this with See's Candies. If Buffett and Munger had not sought out Ira Marshall's advice and bought See's Candies, Berkshire Hathaway would have missed out on a couple of billion dollars in profits.

We saw this with Ray Dalio as well. Earlier, we highlighted one of the investor's biggest failures. To jog your memory, Dalio wrongly predicted that a depression would come. This reason he predicted a depression was that Mexico had recently defaulted on its debts and many other countries had similar levels of debt, making Dalio believe that the other countries would default as well.

Was Dalio's reasoning illogical? Not necessarily.

He saw that Mexico defaulted on its debts. He saw that other countries had similar credit risks. Therefore, he concluded that those countries would likely default. That would sound perfectly logical to most people. It certainly sounded logical to him—a very intelligent man—and the investors who listened to him. Yet, even though his reasoning was logical, he was totally wrong. The Fed and IMF were able to keep the global economy stable, and Dalio's reputation was destroyed in the short-term, "cost[ing] [him] just about everything [he] had built at Bridgewater."

We see this happen all the time in life. We often have lines of reasoning that sound totally logical but are totally off.

Many lay people, for example, think that an actively managed mutual fund would outperform the market. After all, if you are paying a fee, you should get extra value. Moreover, wouldn't someone who is actively studying the markets be able to outperform a fund that literally isn't being managed by anything? Nope. By and large, actively managed funds can't outperform passively managed funds. As we saw in the introduction, about 85% of professional investors don't outperform over a 10-year period. What even surprised me was that many people who literally spend their lives studying Warren Buffett still manage to underperform, as we saw in the introduction.

When investing, you obviously do not want to have a logical train of reasoning that turns out to be wrong. When those occur, they can turn out to be disastrous, as was the case with Ray Dalio and almost the case with Berkshire Hathaway.

So, what follows is a strategy to think clearly—a strategy from an Outlier Individual: Elon Musk.

THINK USING FIRST PRINCIPLES

During my sophomore year of college, I was looking for marketing and finance internships to gain some experience.[17] I knew that I

---

17   Some readers might be wondering why someone who writes books on investing would want an internship in marketing. Well, at the time, I wanted to work at a firm that employed a Warren Buffett style of investing. But it was hard to find any such firms that I admired and that had a good performance track record. Marketing served as a backup career path for me.

was a standout candidate for the roles that I was applying to, especially for the finance roles. By my sophomore year, I had already written a couple of books about investing, which I knew would impress recruiters.

When crafting my resume, I was extra careful about following every single resume rule. I made sure that the formatting was professional. All my bullet points started with active verbs. I quantified my bullet points. I highlighted the "impact" of my experiences at the end of every bullet point.

Then, I had it read by a couple of people. They felt confident that my resume was strong, so I started applying mainly to finance internships, though I did apply to select marketing roles that sounded interesting.

At first, I thought that getting an internship at a good company would be a piece of cake. In a sense, I knew that I had a competitive advantage. There weren't many college sophomores who could say that they had written a book, especially on a topic that's related to the job. Of course, I'm not saying that I was overqualified or "too good for the job." The books I had written at the time were just introductory level books for new investors, so they didn't make me overqualified for any role. But, in my opinion, writing those books conveyed my passion for investing and finance.

Knowing that I had a good chance at standing out, I applied to just a small handful of internships at the beginning of the school year. I was fairly confident that I didn't need to apply to very many roles. In fact, that's what had worked the previous year. During my freshman year, I didn't apply to more than 10-15 internships, but I managed to land one at a private equity firm. So, I said to myself, "It won't take that many applications to land an internship. After all, last year it didn't take many applications. And now, I have a relevant internship, I've taken more finance classes, and I have a stronger resume, so it should be easier to land an internship."

After submitting my resumes, I waited one week to hear back from the companies. I received no responses.

I waited another week. I still received no responses.

I waited a month. I still received no responses.

I waited two more months, and I still received no responses.

At that point, I realized that I wasn't going to get any responses from those companies.[18]

To get more responses, I decided to reflect on what I did wrong. I first re-reviewed my resume several times. Again, I made sure that I was following resume best practices, such as using active verbs, quantifying outcomes, and removing grammar errors. Moreover, I made sure that I was actually applying for jobs for which I was a good fit.

So, I started to apply to jobs again. I decided to apply to more jobs (about 100-200). Applying to more roles would ensure that I had a handful of interviews. I also decided to tailor my resume to the job descriptions of each role, which I was told would increase my chances of my resume feeling like a good fit.

At this point, I felt like my chances of landing many interviews was quite high. After all, what could go wrong? I had great resumes that were tailored to each position, and I had a sustainable competitive advantage due to my books.

However, I had nearly the same results as before.

I waited one week. I received no responses.

I waited another week. I still received no responses.

I waited a month. I still received no responses.

I waited two more months, and I ended up with a couple of responses—but for roles that I wasn't too interested in (which I ended up getting rejected from after the interview phase).

I was honestly disappointed with the results. I thought I would get a lot of interviews, but I barely got any.

I didn't know exactly what to do at this point. I could have applied to more roles, but that felt like a waste of time. I probably

---

18   To be technically correct, one of the companies I applied to ended up inviting me to an interview many, many months later. They were looking specifically for someone who had a deep interest in Warren Buffett's investment philosophy. I felt like a strong candidate for the role because I enjoyed writing books that covered Warren Buffett's investment philosophy—like this one. Yet, I didn't end up getting a call back after a first-round interview.

wouldn't have ended up with many responses by doing more of what I was already doing. I also couldn't see anything wrong with my resume.

So, I decided to take a break from submitting job applications. I would apply to internships here and there, but I was mainly focusing on other things: doing well in school, writing books, and building skills for internships.

However, when I was on a break one day, I had a critical breakthrough.

Just by chance, I came across a YouTube video that sounded interesting. It was called "The First Principles Method Explained by Elon Musk." As the title suggests, it was a video of Elon Musk explaining a problem-solving technique called First Principles thinking, which allows him to develop innovative and superb products.

In the video, he says that there are two ways of thinking. People can either reason by analogy, or they can reason by first principles, both of which I'll quickly explain.

Reasoning by analogy is what I call reasoning by comparison. It is "a specific way of thinking, based on the idea that because two or more things are similar in some respects, they are probably also similar in some further respect." In other words, if two things are similar in one respect, people think that they are similar in another manner.

An example of reasoning by analogy is "Warren Buffett buys companies with strong competitive advantages, and he has outperformed the market. Therefore, if a retail investor buys companies with sustainable competitive advantages, they will outperform the market." This is an example of reasoning by analogy because the statement...

- Identifies a similarity between Buffett's and the retail investor's strategy ("If they both buy companies with sustainable competitive advantages")

- Concludes that Buffett and the retail investor must be similar in another manner ("Then, the retail investor must outperform")

The problem with reasoning by analogy is that you can sustain incorrect arguments when you do so. For example, when cars were first created, many people didn't believe that they would replace horses. Why? Well, they saw that America had plenty of grass through the years when horses were around. They also noticed that grass was going to continue to be around for many years. In other words, they noticed that, even with the invention of cars, the world would still be similar in one respect: it would still have plenty of grass. So, they concluded that the world would be similar in another respect: they assumed horses would continue to be used in the future. "Grass is still going to be around, so why would horses go away?" As Elon Musk once highlighted the arguments of pro-horse individuals,

> You can't say...'Nobody wants a car because horses are great and we're used to them and they can eat grass, there's lots of grass all over the place. And— you know—there's no gasoline that people can buy, so people are never going to get cars.' People did say that.

Reasoning by first principles, on the other hand, is really the opposite of reasoning by analogy.

It involves breaking down a situation into its fundamental truths and then drawing conclusions based on those truths. To illustrate this, let me give you an example.

Many people used to reason by analogy and tell Elon Musk that electric vehicle battery packs would always be too expensive at $600 per kilowatt hour. They had a very logical reason for that. The cost of battery packs had been $600 per kilowatt hour or higher since their existence, and that price wasn't falling. Therefore, people concluded that it wouldn't cost less than $600 per kilowatt hour in the future.

But Elon Musk proved them wrong. He said that it is a fundamental truth that batteries are made of cobalt, nickel, aluminum, carbon, polymers, and a steel can. (Without these materials, you can't make a battery). Then, he said, it is a fundamental truth that it would cost less than $600 per kilowatt hour if one could figure out how to combine those items in the shape of a battery for less than $600 per kilowatt hour. Therefore, he concluded that it was possible for batteries to be manufactured for less than $600 per kilowatt hour. And he did that.

What reasoning by first principles does is make your line of reasoning true.

In an earlier chapter, we said that your mind is only as good as the data it has; if your mind has lots of accurate data on why businesses succeed and fail, it is much more likely to make accurate predictions.

Examples of reasoning by analogy	
Similarity	**Conclusion**
Warren Buffett and a retail investor both buy companies with sustainable competitive advantages	The retail investor will outperform the stock market
The world had plenty of grass before 1886, when the first car was invented. The world will continue to have lots of grass after 1886.	Horses will remain the dominant type of transportation after 1886 because the world still has grass
Many resumes that land an interview have lots of numbers. My resumes also has lots of numbers.	My resume will land an interview

Examples of reasoning by first principles	
Fundamental truth	**Conclusion**
Stocks purchased below intrinsic value will outperform	The retail investor will only outperform if they purchase stocks below intrinsic value
Consumers prefer products that are higher-quality	Consumers will prefer to use cars over horses
Resumes that are impressive and relevant will land an interview	My resume won't land an interview unless it's impressive and relevant

The same concept applies with reasoning from first principles. Your conclusions are only as good as the assumptions they are based upon. If the underlying assumptions are true, then there is a good chance that your conclusions will be good as well. You won't be right 100% of the time, but there is a far higher chance that your conclusions will be right if your assumptions are right.

That's why reasoning by first principles works. Remember, reasoning by first principles is about starting with fundamental, undeniable assumptions about the way the world works. Then, you're using those true assumptions to draw conclusions. Going back to a previous example, reasoning by first principles wouldn't be saying that "battery packs will be expensive in the future because they have been expensive in the past." It's not fundamentally true that something will be expensive in the future because it has been expensive in the past; that's not a true assumption. Therefore, you would draw incorrect conclusions if you relied on that assumption. On the other hand, reasoning by first principles would involve saying, "batteries are made of cobalt, nickel, aluminum, carbon, polymers, and a steel can" and "we can reduce the cost of a battery if we can combine those items in the shape of a battery pack in a cheaper manner." Both of those statements are fundamentally true. Therefore, if you rely on them to draw conclusions, your conclusions will likely hold true.

In fact, applying first principles thinking to resume writing completely changed the quality of my resume.

After watching Elon Musk explain first principles reasoning, I realized that I was reasoning by analogy when creating my resume.

I saw that many successful applicants quantified everything on their resume, so I thought my resume would be strong if I quantified everything.

I saw that many successful applicants used active verbs, so I thought my resume would be strong if I used active verbs.

I saw that many successful applicants ensured that their bullet points highlighted their impact, so I thought my resume would be strong if my bullet points conveyed an impact.

But, if you think about it, those are not fundamental truths about the way the world works.

Of course, a resume looks more professional if it has a lot of numbers. But it is not an undeniable, fundamental truth that a resume will land an interview if it has a bunch of numbers on it. Virtually all candidates quantify everything on their resume. Yet, most of them won't be invited to an interview.

A resume looks more professional if the bullet points highlight impacts. But it is not an undeniable, fundamental truth that a resume will land an interview if it highlights a bunch of impacts. Once again, virtually all candidates highlight the impacts of their actions. Yet, most of them aren't invited back to an interview.

The same can be said for using active verbs. Active verbs look better than passive verbs. But it is not an undeniable, fundamental truth that a resume will land an interview if it has active verbs. Then everyone would end up landing interviews.

Knowing the advantages of first principles thinking, then, I decided to take the Elon Musk approach to creating a resume. I decided to break down resume-writing into its first principles. In particular, I realized that it was a fundamental truth that a resume would land an interview if it did two things.

First, it had to sound relevant. It was virtually an undeniable truth that a resume would get rejected if it didn't seem relevant to the role. If you submit a finance resume to a computer science role, it will get rejected. So, I knew that my resume had to sound relevant.

Second, it had to sound impressive—extremely impressive. I was highly certain that a resume that sounded far more impressive than that of other candidates would land an interview. If resume A sounded very impressive while resume B didn't, I knew that resume A would almost always beat out resume B (assuming that both resumes were relevant).

Armed with those two first principles, I went back to writing a resume. This time, however, I didn't optimize it to "have a lot of numbers" or to "highlight impacts." Instead, I just made it sound impressive and relevant.

For example, I knew that writing and marketing books was more impressive than the work I had done in various clubs. So, I did something extreme. With two exceptions, I removed all my experiences from my resume except the work I did on my books. I knew that the work I did on my books was more impressive than many of the clubs I was in, so why not have that be the focus of my resume as long as I could make it relevant?

Of course, that change broke major resume-writing rules. The common rule of thumb is that each experience should have 6-10 lines of bullet points. I had nearly 30 lines devoted to my book.

And I broke many more resume writing rules as well. In some cases, I highlighted "what I did" over "my impact" because I thought "what I did" was more impressive than "the impact." I reduced the number of statistics in my resume because I didn't think some of them sounded impressive. In fact, I used the first person in one bullet point, which people advise you should never do.

But I was comfortable breaking the rules. According to my first principles logic, resumes that are relevant and impressive have a very high probability of getting an applicant an interview. Therefore, I knew that I was making good changes as long as they made my resume more relevant and impressive—even if I was blatantly breaking resume-writing rules.

The changes ended up making a big difference.

In one instance, the resume changes landed me an interview for a marketing internship at a large company. I told myself, "Great! Writing an impressive and relevant resume got me past the resume screening phase. Now, I just need to be impressive and relevant during the HR screening interview."

So, I did that. I talked about my most impressive accomplishments related to marketing my previous books. For example, I mentioned that, for at least a year, *Buffett's 2-Step Stock Market Strategy* was one of the highest selling books in the USA and Canada on how to value a publicly traded company. I talked about how I had run ad campaigns that had gathered, at the time, about 15,000,000 impressions. I talked about how I had managed professional publishing teams where several individuals had more than a decade's worth of work experience.

That worked—sort of. The recruiter loved my experiences. But she loved them too much. She gave me a call back saying that "You sounded a bit too overqualified for the internship position, so we didn't think it made sense for you to accept an internship-level position from a career perspective. But, if a more senior level position opens up, I'll give you a call if you're qualified for the role." Though I didn't land the role, I wasn't upset with that outcome.

In another instance, I was in an interview for a consulting internship at a boutique consulting firm. The interviewer read my resume for the first time during the interview. He read the first bullet point and said, "Wow! You wrote a book?" He read the second bullet point and said, "How did you sell that many books?" He read the third bullet point and (I think jokingly) said, "You proved that the book marketing strategy created by a consultant from a big 3 management consulting firm was bound to fail? You must be the best candidate for this job."

By the end of the interview, he was so sold on me that my strategy of "sounding impressive" almost backfired. He said, "If there is ever a very big red flag in someone, I've always believed that you should just ask them up front." He went on to ask, "Do you even want this job? What you've done in writing is very impressive, so why not become a writer?" In response, I told him, honestly, that "none of my books have a sustainable competitive advantage, so it wouldn't be a smart idea to pursue writing full time at this point. Moreover, I don't make enough from writing books to feel good about doing it full time."

That convinced him that I was a good candidate for the role. A few weeks later, I received a call from HR saying that all my interviewers were "very impressed" and that I had received an offer. However, that offer was for the following summer, not the upcoming summer, and I still wanted an internship for the upcoming summer. So, I kept looking.

Later on, I saw that a big 3 management consulting firm was looking for a marketing intern to work within their publishing team.

I knew that I would be the perfect candidate for the role. They were looking for someone who had a passion for marketing, writing, and publishing, especially about business topics. I was probably the only intern candidate who had written business books before (and probably one of the only people in the department who had a bestselling business book under my belt). As mentioned earlier, I also had experience leading late-career publishing professionals who formerly worked at leading publishers like Penguin Random House, and I had experience running somewhat large ad campaigns to promote my books. What kind of recruiter wouldn't like those kinds of experiences for a publishing internship?

However, I still knew that I wouldn't have landed the position without having a referral. The firm I was applying to was highly selective, and it had a reputation of essentially hiring Ivy League students with top GPAs. I had good grades, but no Ivy League background.

So, I decided to network with individuals at the company. I reached out to a couple of very friendly alumni of my school who worked at the firm—Rafi S. and Kimberly B.—to help me get in touch with the right people, and I cold emailed a couple of dozen people. At one point, I even diverted a small portion of my book marketing budget towards running LinkedIn ad campaigns that targeted everyone in the company's publishing department.

Eventually, I ended up getting in touch with a manager, Heather H., within the company's publishing department, and I was able to schedule a networking call with her.

Once again, I went back to first principles. I knew that it was fundamentally true that I would be an attractive candidate if I sounded relevant and impressive. During the networking call, then, I talked a lot about my most impressive writing experiences, and I tried to ask a lot of impressive questions about her experience in writing.

That worked—sort of.

She ended up referring me for the internship.

But, during the call, I learned that the interns couldn't actually do any writing work because, within her specific team, working as a writer required 10 years of writing experience and (ideally) a master's degree in journalism, while I was only a college sophomore pursuing a bachelor's degree in finance and marketing. Instead, the intern was expected to simply do website search engine optimization.

However, the manager I was networking with sounded as if she really liked me and my passion for writing books. Towards the end of the call, she said that she would let me take on a writing role within her team, assuming that I did a good job with the SEO responsibilities and that I had some supervision. In essence, I had used first principles thinking to not only get a referral for a competitive internship, but to also convince someone to be okay with me working in a role that required 10 years of work experience and a degree that I had never taken a class on.

Yet, in the end, I didn't end up even getting an interview for the writing internship, even with a strong referral and a best-selling book under my belt. By the time summer came along, I had convinced a couple of firms that I was a strong candidate for slightly senior level positions, but, ironically, no one wanted me for an intern level role for the upcoming summer. Without a summer internship, I decided to do a passion project over the summer: write *Outlier Investors*.

APPLYING FIRST PRINCIPLES TO INVESTING

If you take a look at history, you'll notice that some of the most inaccurate investment predictions were made due to investors reasoning by analogy.

Take the story of John Antioco as an example.

In 1997, Antioco was looking for a job. As a late-career business professional, he was applying to become the CEO of various companies.

In particular, he was looking to become the CEO of a company that had a lot of potential to be successful. Like most CEOs, he knew that it would be a bad idea to take a job at a company unless he knew that it would be successful. If he joined a company that performed poorly, people would blame him for the company's poor performance, materially hurting his future job prospects.

After looking hard, he came across a company that sounded as if it had a lot of potential for many reasons. He "liked the brand." The company was the largest player in its niche, indicating that it was highly competitive. At the same time, it only had 25% market share. This meant that 75% of the market wasn't owned by the company, indicating that there was a lot of potential to grow the company. Moreover, there were several small issues in the company that could be "fixed quickly," which could quickly boost profits for shareholders.

Recognizing the potential in the company, John Antioco decided to apply to become the CEO, and he landed the role.

As predicted, the company was successful. For example, after joining, Antioco saw that the company had a problem. Its inventory costs were too high at $65 per unit, preventing the company from being able to buy enough inventory to fulfill demand. So, to reduce inventory costs, Antioco formed a revenue sharing agreement with its suppliers. Under the agreement, the company only had to pay $1 per unit, but it had to give 40% of its revenues to its suppliers in return. Although it had to give away 40% of its sales, the company was able to fulfill a larger portion of consumer demand because it could buy more inventory at $1 per unit than it could at $65 per unit. The new supplier agreement contributed to revenue growing from $4.4 billion to $5.9 billion between 1999 and 2003.

Given Antioco's success, there was no question that many things were going well.

Until they weren't.

What I haven't told you yet, in this chapter, is that John Antioco wasn't the CEO of just any company. He was the CEO of Blockbuster, a company that was on the verge of collapse. A few years after he joined, Antioco faced stiff competitive pressures from Netflix, which had developed a better business model. Netflix distributed its movies by shipping them to consumers, while Blockbuster was mainly reliant on an in-store strategy, allowing Netflix to be closer to the end consumer. As a result, Netflix was able to quickly take market share from Blockbuster, causing sales to decline.

The situation got so dire that Antioco himself stopped believing in Blockbuster. After leaving the company in 2007, Antioco sold all his Blockbuster stock and bought into Netflix at $20 per share because he "could see that Netflix was going to have the whole DVD-by-mail market handed to it."

What's interesting about Blockbuster is that the CEO was incredibly incorrect about the company's future. When Antioco joined Blockbuster in 1997, he believed that it had a significant "opportunity" to grow market share and assert dominance. He "didn't believe that technology would threaten Blockbuster as fast as critics thought." But the exact opposite happened. Blockbuster ended up declaring bankruptcy just a little over 10 years after Antioco joined.

There are many reasons why Antioco could have misjudged Blockbuster's long-term competitiveness.

One reason could be that Antioco was only thinking about the short term. That would be a very fair possibility since Antioco had a history of doing short-term, turnaround projects. For example, before joining Blockbuster, Antioco was the CEO of Taco Bell for just eight months, where he was tasked with turning around the company's streak of declining sales. Before joining Taco Bell, he worked in a couple of executive positions at Circle K for five years, a fairly short period of time. Moreover, his goal at Circle K wasn't to devise a long-term strategy. Instead, it was to simply figure out how to quickly take it out of bankruptcy, which he successfully did when he sold the company by the end of his tenure. Therefore, Antioco had a history of staying at companies for a short period of time. So, when applying to Blockbuster, he could have only been thinking about its short-term prospects.

Another possible cause of Antioco's miscalculation is simply that predicting the future is hard. When an industry is undergoing a lot of change, people tend to find it harder to predict its future. If you had to decide whether Coca-Cola or Meta is easier to predict, you would most likely say Coca-Cola is easier to predict. Why? Coca-Cola's business doesn't change much from year to year, decreasing the potential variation in outcomes. Blockbuster's industry, on the other hand, had a very wide range of outcomes because competitors were experimenting with entirely new business models and capitalizing on new technologies. Therefore, anyone—including Antioco—may have had a difficult time predicting the future of Blockbuster.

However, I would argue that there is a deeper reason why Antioco miscalculated Blockbuster's future. I believe that Antioco's prediction of Blockbuster would have been more accurate had he reasoned by first principles.

A first principles investor (or CEO) would have said, "It is a fundamental truth that businesses with A, B, and C characteristics will be the most successful." For example, they may have realized that some of the following are fundamental truths of consumer behavior:

- Consumers love items that are cheaper, assuming quality is held constant.
- Consumers love to deal with businesses that are easier to buy from.
- Consumers love having a selection.
- Consumers gravitate towards companies that have strong brands (assuming they have a competitive product).
- Consumers love phenomenal customer experiences.

Then, a first principles investor would have used those principles to predict which businesses would be successful. They would have asked themselves, "who will be able to offer the lowest prices? Will Blockbuster be the easiest company for consumers to buy from? Will Blockbuster be able to provide a better customer experience than upcoming companies like Netflix? A first principles investor would feel comfortable predicting Blockbuster's future only after answering those questions.

However, based on publicly available information, Antioco didn't follow a first principles approach when analyzing Blockbuster.

Let's revisit his reasons for joining the company.

One of the reasons Antioco joined Blockbuster was the large potential to grow market share. In his own words, "Blockbuster was by far the biggest video rental company, but its market share was only 25%. To me, that was an opportunity."

Antioco's argument, on the surface, sounds perfectly logical. Not owning 75% of the market means that there is a lot of market available to take from competitors. Hence, there is a lot of opportunity to grow sales, increasing the probability of being successful.

However, it is important to note that Antioco was reasoning by analogy and not by first principles.

Like Antioco, many people notice that many extremely successful companies—such as Amazon, Apple, and Coca-Cola—chased after large market opportunities. Amazon disrupted the entire retail industry, an industry so large that it includes competitors like Walmart and Target. Apple created a product that's now in the hands of over 1 billion consumers. Coca-Cola tapped such a large market that it was able to sell over a billion 8-ounce servings of cola every day.

Knowing that many successful businesses pursued large markets, people then tend to believe that business ventures that pursue a larger market will be more successful. In other words, they end up saying things like, "We should pursue business opportunities with large market potentials because many successful businesses pursued large market opportunities."

Of course, we know that it is not a fundamental truth that a business will succeed if it is pursuing a larger market opportunity. There are many counter examples to prove that.

Consider the dot com companies. All the companies in the dotcom bubble were pursuing large market opportunities. Did that mean that they had a large potential to grow? No. They were never able to sustainably deliver better products to consumers.

Conversely, it is not fundamentally true that a product won't sell merely because the market is small.

Consider Tesla. There wasn't a large market for electric vehicles in the early 2010s. According to the International Energy Agency, there were only 20,000 registered electric vehicles in the USA in 2011. Many people, therefore, said, "Elon Musk isn't smart for starting Tesla. Even if it is successful, Elon Musk won't sell many cars because the market is small. On top of that, consumers are largely preferring sticking with gasoline vehicles, so the market won't be large enough in the future." Of course, in hindsight, those people were very wrong. To date, Tesla has sold over 1.9 million electric vehicles.

People were wrong about Tesla back then because they weren't reasoning by first principles. As I just mentioned, people would say, "It's impossible for Tesla to sell more than 500,000 electric cars because the market size is only 20,000 vehicles, and many consumers aren't flocking towards electric vehicles. Therefore, the market will not be big enough in the future." As we know now, however, that's not a fundamentally true statement. The evidence is right in front of you with Tesla's sales. What is fundamentally true is that consumers like products that deliver more pleasure than alternatives. If Tesla can create a car that people prefer over gasoline ones, they will buy it. If not, they won't buy it. So, even if the market size was only 20,000 cars and even if the market wasn't growing that dramatically on a unit basis in the early 2010s, it didn't matter to Tesla's sales. What mattered was how much consumers liked the product. If the market was 20,000 cars and Tesla suddenly created a car that consumers preferred over gasoline cars, Elon Musk would have sold far more than 20,000 cars. And that's exactly what happened.

Therefore, if you were attempting to predict Tesla's future back in 2010, the question that you shouldn't have been asking yourself was, "what is the industry size and growth rate?" That wouldn't have led to accurate guesses about Tesla's future; the only conclusion you would have had was that Tesla was mathematically bound to fail. What you would have wanted to recognize was the fundamental truth that people buy great products. Then, you would have wanted to ask yourself, "what will Tesla's product quality be in the future? How will it compare to the competition's products? How long will it take for Tesla to develop such a product?" Thinking about Tesla's future product quality would have been the best approach to predicting Tesla's future in 2010 because product quality fundamentally determines sales—while market size doesn't.

The same concept applies to Blockbuster. When analyzing Blockbuster, a first principles investor would have said, "it is not fundamentally true that a business will succeed merely because the market is large. Instead, it is fundamentally true that a business will be successful if it has well-marketed products that consumers love." Had Antioco done that, he would have realized that Blockbuster was unlikely to succeed over the long term. He would have seen that the competition was more innovative than Blockbuster, allowing them to develop a better product over the long term and defeat Block-buster. Moreover, he would have realized that the fact that the market opportunity was large was, to a certain extent, irrelevant because it doesn't fundamentally determine the sales of a business.

Reasoning by analogy even caused early analysts of Amazon to miss out on a great investment opportunity.

They noticed that many tech stocks failed during the dotcom bubble. So, they concluded that Amazon was likely to fail since it was also a tech stock. Of course, a lot of tech stocks did fail during the dotcom bubble. But it isn't fundamentally true that a business will fail because it is a tech company.

They noticed that many businesses that have tried to compete directly against established incumbents have failed. So, they said that Amazon was too risky because it was competing against firms like Walmart. Of course, it is hard to compete against an incumbent. But it isn't fundamentally true that a company will fail if it has large competitors. Fundamentally, a company fails because it is less competitive than competitors, not because the competition is competitive. If you used that train of logic in every industry, it obviously wouldn't hold. In that case, you could argue that every company in a competitive industry—Apple, Facebook, Google, Geico, See's Candies, Exxon Mobil, Goldman Sachs, Pepsi—will fail.

Early Amazon analysts noticed that many businesses with a history of stable cash flows are safe businesses. So, they concluded that Amazon wasn't a safe business since it didn't have a history of producing stable cash flows. Of course, having a long history of stable profits can be a predictor of a company's safety. But as we talked about in one of the first chapters, it isn't fundamentally true that a business is unsafe if its cash flows are unstable, nor is it true that a business is safe because its cash flows are stable. By that logic, you could argue that many oil companies are speculative because all oil companies don't produce stable cash flows. In fact, I would guarantee that many of the people who said that "Amazon is risky because it doesn't product consistent cash flows" also owned shares in oil companies and other commodity businesses.

Reasoning by analogy caused those analysts to engage in a mental bias which I call Weighing the Analogies.

Typically, people like to make decisions by weighing the pros and cons or the risks and rewards. Many professional investors, for example, build financial models to estimate the price of a stock if things go well and the price of a stock if things go poorly. Then, they decide to invest based on whether they think the upside potential of a stock is greater than the downside potential. Similarly, many retail investors like to write down the pros and cons of an investment decision before investing in a company.

Weighing pros and cons can be a good way to make decisions in some situations. But, when you are trying to predict the future of a company, it isn't always the best idea to weigh pros and cons.

When most people weigh pros and cons, they are typically weighing factors that are derived from reasoning by analogy.

The early analysts of Amazon, for example, thought it was a con that Amazon was a tech company, even though it isn't fundamentally true that a tech company is bad.

They thought it was a major con that Amazon was competing against major competitors, even though it isn't fundamentally true that a company will fail if it has large competitors.

They thought that it was a con that Amazon didn't have stable cash flows, even though it isn't fundamentally true that a company is bad because its cash flows aren't stable.

Then, the analysts stacked all those cons (and many more) against the few pros. So, they concluded it must be a bad business.

Now, that approach may have sounded logical. But it really wasn't.

Those cons didn't really matter at the end of the day. Although Amazon faced stiff competition, they built a better product. Although they were a tech company, they overcame the adversities faced by other tech companies. And although cash flows weren't stable initially, they managed to build a cash flow behemoth.

The reason that those cons didn't matter was that they just weren't based on first principles. Had the analysts been focusing on first principles, they would have been focusing on factors that undeniably matter to a company's success—things like customer experience. In that case, they would have had better chances of being right about Amazon.

In fact, that's exactly what Jeff Bezos did. Despite all the cons, Jeff Bezos believed that Amazon had a "good chance" of succeeding. How he knew that was simple. He went to first principles. In 1999—when many investors would have simply said that Amazon was just a tech company that was bound to fail—he recognized that it was undeniably true that a company that creates a far better product for customers would succeed, even against many headwinds:

> If you can focus obsessively enough on customer experience—selection, ease of use, low prices, more information to make purchase decision with—if you can give customers all of that... then I think you have a good chance [at succeeding].

What you'll find in the investment world, however, is that investors rarely invest on first principles.

Not very long ago, an investor was telling me about his investment philosophy.

Overall, his investment philosophy, within reason, made sense to me. Just like Warren Buffett, he liked to buy stocks that had strong competitive advantages. As many investors recommend, he had a mindset of being "greedy when others are fearful and fearful when others are greedy." On top of that, as with Lou Simpson and Mohnish Pabrai, he preferred to minimize diversification to maximize returns. So far, his investment philosophy made sense to me.

However, that all changed when he started to explain how he evaluated management teams. When evaluating management, he said that he likes to look for management teams that "buy back stock, increase dividends, and have environmental, social, and governance (ESG) initiatives."

But that approach to evaluating management teams didn't make much sense to me.

Of course, it's nice to know that a management team is buying back stock and paying dividends. And it is *definitely* a good thing to see that a management team is employing environmental, social, and governance initiatives.

But it's not fundamentally true that a management team is good if they are buying back stock, paying dividends, and implementing ESG initiatives.

Was Bezos buying back a bunch of stock in 1999? No. Amazon was spending $0 on stock buybacks at the time. Yet Bezos was an incredible manager.

When Steve Jobs returned as Apple's CEO in 1997, was he focusing his attention on ESG initiatives? No, not really. But did that make him a bad manager? Not really, unless you want to argue that the creator of the iPhone was a bad manager.

Or consider The Restaurant, the company I profiled in the chapter called "The Problem of the Annual Report." That management team was spending hundreds of millions of dollars on stock buybacks in some years, and tens of millions of dollars on dividends in other years. On top of that, they were implementing many ESG initiatives. But were they a good management team? Of course not. They managed to diminish the company's long-term sales and brand strength. The Restaurant's competitors didn't hurt its long-term sales. The actions of the management team did so.

In fact, so many investors evaluate management teams based on ideas that aren't fundamentally true. Countless people say, "a management team is good if they are appropriately compensated, don't use the word EBITDA, and have a good board of directors."[19] Yet, there are so many counter examples to suggest that those statements aren't fundamentally true.

---

19   EBITDA (or earnings before interests, taxes, depreciation, and amortization) is a commonly metric used by Wall Street analysts. Investors such as Warren Buffett and Charlie Munger are frequently said to be wary of managers that use EBITDA as a measure of profit. In short, it's an inflated profitability figure that some managements use to make their company look more profitable than it really is.

Remember Ron Johnson? He was the guy who destroyed JCPenney. He, in my view, had a decent board. Bill Ackman, an activist who had a good track record turning around companies, was on it. Ron Johnson was appropriately compensated. In fact, Bill Ackman once stated in an interview that a reason he liked the decision to hire Ron Johnson was that his compensation scheme aligned him directly with shareholders' interests. And Ron Johnson rarely ever used the term EBITDA. In JCPenney's Q4 2012 earnings call, for example, Ron Johnson didn't even use the term EBITDA once. But did that make him a good manager? No. His turnaround strategy destroyed the company's sales.

To properly evaluate a management team, then, you want to start with what's fundamentally true. Then, you want to reason up from there.

I think we can all agree that a management team is good if they maximize shareholder value while acting in an honest, ethical, and moral manner. That, in my view, will always be fundamentally true. I don't think that you would find a single person who would argue that a management team isn't good if they are maximizing shareholder value in an ethical manner.[20]

If you start with that fundamental truth—the truth that a management team is good if they maximize shareholder value while acting in an honest manner—you'll be able to evaluate management teams in a more nuanced and accurate manner.

Consider this personal example. If you asked me whether Elon Musk was a good CEO before I understood first principles thinking, I would have said, "yeah, he's a good guy. After all, he has a lot

---

20   An idea that's gaining popularity in corporate finance is that of stakeholder value. Unlike shareholder value, which represents the value of a company's stock, stakeholder value represents the value of all of a company's stakeholders: suppliers, customers, employees, etc. Some people say that the job of a management team isn't to maximize shareholder value. Instead, they say that their job is to maximize stakeholder value. Personally, like many others, I believe that *long-term* shareholder value cannot be maximized if long-term stakeholder value isn't maximized. Therefore, the idea of maximizing shareholder value isn't in conflict with the idea of maximizing stakeholder value.

of passion for his business. He's clearly smarter than 95% of CEOs in the world. And he's growing sales." That's frankly how many people would evaluate CEOs. They ask themselves, "Is this CEO passionate about running the business? Are they smarter than other CEOs? And are they ensuring that the company's financial statements are healthy?"

But as soon as I started to think in terms of first principles, I started to think differently. I said, "It is fundamentally true that a good CEO maximizes the long-term value of the business. In Coca-Cola's case, that would involve ensuring that the brand is strong over the long-term. But I know that the same isn't true for Tesla. I know that Musk has said many times that Tesla isn't successful because of its marketing and branding strategies. (In fact, I just read an article the other day that said he got rid of Tesla's entire PR department because he didn't think that they were important). Instead of focusing on PR and branding, Musk believes that product quality is what wins at the end of the day—especially in an innovative industry. So, to evaluate whether he is a good CEO, I should focus on his ability to create a good product. That's simply what matters in Musk's business."

"Now, I know that there is no question of whether Tesla has a great product today. Just talk to customers, and they will say that they want it more than most other cars. But to really know whether Musk is a good CEO, I need to know whether Tesla will continue to have a phenomenal product in the future. Whether they will out-innovate competitors, then, is the key question."

"I remember that, earlier, I was watching a video of Tesla's Chief Designer explaining Tesla's culture, and I learned that Musk created a unique culture at Tesla: all the upper-level managers are required to reason by first principles when creating an innovative product. In other words, all key Tesla employees are trained in the same framework Musk uses to create innovative products. That means that Tesla is essentially filled with people who are specifically trained in how to create innovative products."

Then, everything clicked to me.

What makes Musk a good CEO is not merely that can create a good product. It's not merely that he has a passion for his business. Nor is it that he is smart. Instead, it is that he can develop a culture that allows employees to think critically and develop innovative products on their own.

In my view, Tesla would be worthless without that culture. Just think about it. Imagine what would happen if Tesla's employees didn't know how to develop innovative products on their own. If that were the case, Musk would need to constantly micromanage everyone to ensure that they did their job right. That, of course, isn't possible. Tesla has over 50,000 employees. He physically cannot check on every one of them.[21] That means that the only way Tesla can succeed is if they know how to create innovative products without constant oversight by Musk. Therefore, if Tesla didn't have a culture that allowed employees to understand how to develop innovative products, the company probably wouldn't be successful at all. In fact, leadership expert Jocko Willink and the author of *Extreme Ownership* once said that Musk is successful because he knows how to create innovative products without micromanaging his employees:

> [Musk] is successful because he doesn't get stuck down there. Because if he felt the need to micromanage each and every part on a Tesla... it would be very unlikely that he would have the capacity to do all that.

What's interesting, however, is that very few professional and retail investors ever talk about the culture Musk established. You

---

21   Of course, he can micromanage his direct reports. (And, according to some sources, he does micromanage them to a certain extent). But, even then, there are so many decisions that his direct reports are making that it wouldn't be possible for him to have a say on every single one of them.

could talk to any investor about how they would analyze Tesla, and I would guarantee you that they wouldn't think of analyzing Tesla's culture. You could even talk to the people who have big positions in Tesla's shares, and I would bet that very few of them know anything about its culture.

The reason that everyone overlooks such an important part of Tesla's success is that they reason by analogy. They say, "Every successful entrepreneur is passionate about their business. Therefore, Musk is a great entrepreneur because he is passionate about his business." Or, they say, "The best companies have great products. Therefore, Tesla is a great company because it currently has a great product in the market." Of course, it is not wrong to look for passion in CEOs and to favor companies with great products. In fact, you should do both of those things. But when you reason by analogy, you end up overlooking an incredibly important determinant of Tesla's success: its culture.

On the other hand, when you reason by first principles, you end up uncovering important things such as culture. Someone who reasons by first principles would say, "it is fundamentally true that a company that has a great product today *and* in the future will be successful. What matters, then, is not whether a company has a great product today, but whether they will have a great product in the future. Since Tesla is in an innovative industry, the only way they will have a better product in the future is if they out-innovate competitors. Therefore, a CEO's ability to empower employees to be innovative is just as important as the CEO's passion and the company's current product quality." As Musk says:

> What matters is the pace of innovation. That is the fundamental determinant of competitiveness of any given company.... This is obvious that this would occur with Amazon and Walmart because Walmart's rate of innovation was negligible, and Amazon's was very high. The outcome was obvious a long time ago.

When investing, then, always reason by first principles. Break down a competitive situation into its fundamental truths and then reason up from there. First principles thinking helps you predict the success and failure of businesses more accurately than everyone else. It allows you to spot the Blockbuster before everyone else. Moreover, it helps you evaluate businesses and management teams in a more innovative way than everyone else. It allows you to identify the importance of Tesla's culture, while every investor overlooks it.[22]

Be wary of making investment decisions by assessing the "upside and downside" or the "pros and cons." You're likely reasoning by analogy—which is a certain way to make a poor investment decision.

Instead, invest on first principles. Identify the fundamental reasons why businesses succeed and fail, and then reason up from there.

---

22   Just to be clear, I'm not saying that culture is the only thing that you would need to analyze before deciding whether to invest in Tesla. You would also need to analyze factors such as valuation and the competition. But it would be slightly foolish to invest in Tesla without assessing its culture, an important determinant of its ability to out-innovate competitors.

The 5-Minute Rubric

How long do you think making an investment decision should take? 30 minutes? Five hours? Two weeks? Six months?

You'll find a huge spectrum of answers.

Some investors—particularly retail investors—spend no more than a few days researching a stock. I know of people who bought a stock within 24 hours of hearing its name because they liked the company and because the price was down. In fact, a source that calls itself the "one stop solution to financial inquiries" states that it should only take 2-4 hours to research a company.

Other investors—particularly professional investors—spend a much longer period analyzing a stock. One popular value investment fund, Ariel Investments, is quite detailed with its research. They typically have their analysts write "full-blown" research reports, conduct balance sheet analyses, valuation analyses, and competitive analyses. They have several portfolio management teams look at every stock several times, allowing them to get a diverse set of perspectives. They have a dedicated "devil's advocate" to challenge the current consensus. They talk with management teams to understand a firm's strengths and weaknesses. In the end, their team may end up spending "several months" analyzing a stock.

How long do you think you should spend analyzing a stock? Somewhere closer to two hours or two months? Of course, there is no one right answer. You may spend as much or as little time as you want.

But, if I had to guess, the average retail investor believes that they should spend at least one to two days analyzing a stock. On the other hand, I would guess that professional investors, who tend to be more rigorous, would say that a week is the bare minimum to make an investment decision.

But what's interesting is that some Outlier Investors can make investment decisions in no more than a few hours.

Consider Warren Buffett's acquisition of Larson-Juhl.

On December 3rd, 2001, Warren Buffett received a call from Craig Ponzio, the owner of Larson-Juhl, a company that made custom-made picture frames. Craig was interested in selling his company to Berkshire Hathaway. It was the first time Buffett had heard about the company and likely the industry as well. So, he was coming in with no background knowledge about the company.

Despite not having background knowledge about the company, it only took Buffett a few minutes to know that this was a great investment opportunity, and it only took 90 minutes for him to reach an agreement with the seller:

> Though I had never heard of Larson-Juhl before Craig's call, a few minutes of talking with him made me think we would strike a deal. He was straightforward in describing the business, cared about who bought it, and was realistic as to price. Two days later, Craig and Steve McKenzie, his CEO, came to Omaha and in ninety minutes we reached an agreement.

Or consider Buffett's acquisition of his friend's stock in two companies:

> Jack Ringwalt, a friend of mine who was the controlling shareholder of the two companies, came to my office saying he would like to sell. Fifteen minutes later, we had a deal.

The purchases from Jack Ringwalt and Craig weren't just outliers. It is normal for Buffett to make investment decisions very quickly. For example, Buffett tells people who want to sell their business to Berkshire Hathaway that he can let them know whether he is interested in just 5 minutes:

> We can promise complete confidentiality and a very fast answer—customarily within five minutes—as to whether we're interested.

How do Outlier Investors like Buffett make investment decisions far faster than everyone else? More importantly, how do they spend less time analyzing any particular business than everyone else and still make higher quality decisions than everyone else?

The answer lies in whether you use a 5-minute rubric when analyzing a company.

THE RUBRIC-LESS APPROACH

Most people follow two steps to make an investment decision:

1. Research a business thoroughly

2. Conclude whether the business is a good investment

For example, let's say an investor is planning on investing in Wrigley, the candy company that owns brands like M&M's, Snickers, and Skittles.[23]

If they were following the two steps, they would try and consume as much information as possible about Wrigley. They would

---

23   Note that this is a hypothetical example. An investor can't invest in Wrigley because it is a private company.

read many news articles on Wrigley. They would absorb every detail in Wrigley's investor's presentation. They would read through the company's earnings and understand what's been happening with margins and sales in recent years.

Then, after all that research, they would make an investment.

But that process is highly inefficient from a time perspective. Just think about it.

An average retail investor could realistically spend at least eight hours doing all that research, if they were going deep. Similarly, the average professional investor might spend an entire week conducting such an analysis (of course, these numbers can vary a lot from person to person).

However, it is highly improbable that the first stock anyone will analyze will be the perfect one. So, most investors may need to look through, hypothetically, 30 stocks before coming across the right investment.

Therefore, a retail investor might need to spend 240 hours or ten days analyzing stocks to (maybe) come across one investment (30 multiplied by 8). Similarly, a professional investor may need to spend 1,200 hours or 50 days analyzing stocks to find a sound investment (30 multiplied by 40).

Of course, those are just hypothetical numbers. Some people can screen through securities faster. And other investors may have lower quality standards for stocks, reducing the need to look through as many securities.

But you get the idea. You are going to waste a lot of time if you (1) research the business thoroughly and (2) only then conclude whether it is a good investment.

Moreover, you'll notice that some Outlier Investors don't conduct due diligence into their investments. Unlike how a private equity firm might spend weeks conducting due diligence, Outlier Investors simply don't. Just think about it. Buffett sometimes acquires companies in a matter of minutes. The Larson-Juhl acquisition happened through a 15-minute phone call and a 90-minute meeting with the business owner. Buffett's deal with Jack Ringwalt occurred in just 15 minutes. In such short periods of time, it is not physically possible to conduct due diligence on any company. Even for a team of people, that's not humanly possible.

Thus, when you analyze a stock, you don't want to conduct endless hours of research into it, and, if you work in private equity, you don't want to spend countless weeks conducting due diligence. That's simply not an efficient way to go about analyzing businesses, nor is it the way Outlier Investors go about making investment decisions.

This lesson applies more generally to life as well. When you are making big decisions or solving problems, it's generally not the best idea to read every detail on the topic.

Take the consulting field as an example. Strategy consulting is one of the most popular career paths for Harvard, Stanford, and Wharton MBA graduates.

Why? Because it looks good on a resume. Every employer knows that, once you've worked at a major strategy consulting firm, you're an incredibly talented individual. Strategy consulting acts as a seal of approval on a resume because the job is incredibly difficult. Strategy consultants are generally advising the c-suite executives of the top Fortune 500 companies. Typically, Fortune 500 companies hire strategy consultants to solve problems that are so tough that the company itself doesn't know how to solve them.

What you would expect from a strategy consultant is that they would conduct extremely thorough research before presenting recommendations to the client. Why wouldn't they? After all, they are often advising c-suite executives on major decisions like acquisitions, product launches, and strategy initiatives—things that can make or break a company's success. On top of that, the consultants are usually not very experienced. Often they have just received their undergraduate degree or MBA, and they definitely have less experience than the c-suite executives of the Fortune 500 companies they are advising. Due to their lack of experience, then, you would expect them to conduct extremely thorough research before presenting any sort of recommendation to their clients. After all, how could they solve a complex problem—that c-suite executives can't solve—without actually doing thorough research?

Well, it turns out that strategy consultants don't do incredibly thorough research before presenting their recommendations to the client. Don't take it from me. Take it from Heinrich Rusche, a former strategy consultant who provides training to aspiring consultants. He says that the wrong way to solve a problem is by conducting thorough research:

> And now, what many young graduates and also more inexperienced business professionals will do is that they will say, 'Until I have closed [the] gaps, until I've really looked at everything, until I really did my thorough research, no way I can come up with a solution. Until I did all of this, right?' And this, my friends, is not how you should operate in the business world.

That begs an important question. How do strategy consultants make such big recommendations without conducting thorough research? More importantly, how do people like Buffett make investment decisions without conducting thorough research into their investments?

THE 5-MINUTE RUBRIC APPROACH

When solving problems for their clients, consultants will never research every little detail. Instead, they create a framework or 5-minute rubric for approaching the problem.

Let me give you a simple example that was created by Heinrich Rusche. Let's say that there is a hypothetical payment service provider that is looking to expand into the Brazilian market. The CEO of the company is looking for your opinion on whether it makes sense for them to break into the market.

To come up with a sound recommendation for the CEO, most people would spend hours researching everything about the Brazilian market. They would read the leading industry reports on Brazil, the annual reports of the largest competitors in Brazil, and they would talk to all the best industry experts. Only then, would most people decide.

Consultants, on the other hand, would take a different approach. Before doing any research at all, they would create a framework or 5-minute rubric for evaluating the Brazilian market.

A 5-minute rubric is simply a list of criteria to evaluate a decision. You likely came across rubrics in school. Teachers often provide students with a list of criteria that show how students are graded on a project. That's a rubric.

Or you may have come across rubrics in a hiring setting. In high school, I was applying for a summer job at Walgreens. During the interview, the hiring manager, Marty, had an actual rubric in his hands that was provided by HR. He was required to use the rubric to rate me in areas such as communication and teamwork.

Consultants do the exact same thing. Just as a teacher will create a rubric to evaluate students and a company will create a rubric to evaluate job candidates, a consultant will create a rubric to evaluate the attractiveness of a decision. Continuing with the Brazilian market example, a consultant won't research every nook and cranny of the Brazilian market. Instead, they will create a concise rubric of the three to seven most important criteria that the Brazilian market needs to meet in order for it to make sense to break into it. For example, Heinrich Rusche suggested that a consultant may want to evaluate the Brazilian market across these four criteria:

1. Market growth rate

2. Affinity to mobile payments

3. Attractiveness of the client's offering or service

4. Competitive landscape

Creating a 5-minute rubric is incredibly efficient from a time perspective. Just think about it. Without a rubric, a consultant would end up researching every little detail of the Brazilian market. But that wouldn't even be possible since there is so much information being pumped out on any topic these days. On top of that, consulting projects are sometimes just a few weeks to a few months long. It simply wouldn't be feasible to look into every detail in such a short period. By developing a rubric, however, a consultant can narrow down their research scope. Instead of having to research everything about the decision, they identify the three to seven most important areas to research. Instead of reading everything about the Brazilian markets, a former consultant like Heinrich Rusche would only focus on areas like the market growth rate and the competitive landscape.

In fact, you'll see Outlier Investors create mental rubrics to help them quickly evaluate businesses. As cited earlier, Buffett said in an annual report that he can decide whether he is interested in a business within just five minutes. That caught some people off guard and made them ask themselves, "can Warren Buffett really make investment decisions that quickly?" To get an answer, someone asked Buffett directly how he makes investment decisions that quickly:

> In the annual report, you stated that 'if anyone out there has a good company, like FlightSafety, please let you know, and you'd be glad to look it over and give an answer within five minutes or less'...How can [you] do that?

In response, Buffett explained how he uses filters—which I refer to as rubrics—to make investment decisions incredibly quickly:

> We have a bunch of filters we've developed in our minds over time. We don't say that they're perfect filters. We don't say that those filters don't occasionally leave things out that should get

through. But... they're efficient. And they work just as well as if we spent months and hired experts and did all kinds of things. So, we really can tell you in five minutes whether we're interested in [a business].

Then, Buffett went on to explain how he conducted virtually no due diligence on FlightSafety before acquiring it:

They have 40 or so training centers around the world [and] I'd never set foot on one of them. I'd never been to their headquarters. We never looked at a lease. We never looked at [the] title of the properties. I mean, we don't do all those things. And I will say this: to date, that's never cost us a penny. What costs us money is when we mis-assess the fundamental economic characteristics of the business. But that is something we would not learn by what people generally consider due diligence.... I think most of the people in this room, if they just focused on what made a good business or didn't make a good business, and thought about it for a little while, they could develop a set of filters that would let them, in five minutes, figure out pretty well what made sense and or didn't make sense.

Then, Charlie Munger said that focusing on a few big ideas (or investment criteria) is far better than conducting ultra-deep due diligence:

I've nothing to add except that people underrate the importance of a few simple big ideas.... A few big ideas really work.

Therefore, when investing in companies, you don't want to follow the two-step approach most people take:

1. Research a business thoroughly

2. Conclude whether the business is a good investment

Instead, you want to take the three-step approach that Outlier Investors take:

1. Create a 5-minute rubric by identifying what's important in a business

2. Research only what's important

3. Draw a conclusion only based on what's important

An Outlier Investor wouldn't seek out every bit of information on Wrigley if they were thinking about investing in it. Instead, they would first create a 5-minute rubric that defines what factors matter in the business—a list of the most important factors an investor would need to analyze before investing in the company. In the case of Wrigley, the rubric may include factors like product quality, brand strength, and distribution strength. Then, they would evaluate the business against the criteria on their rubric. Finally, they would invest in the business if it meets the criteria on their rubric.

As mentioned earlier, this method is far more efficient from a time perspective. With this method, you don't need to read every detail about a company. You don't need to know every piece of news about a company, and you don't need to know every single one of its financial metrics. Instead, you only need to know what's important. So, instead of spending weeks or months analyzing a business, you only need to spend between five minutes and two hours getting a few critical pieces of information.

Most people would point out that there is a clear downside to not conducting deep due diligence: you'll make a poorer decision. "If I know less about a company, surely I'll make poorer decisions. After all, efficient market theory says that investors with more information about a company have an advantage over investors that don't."

I would argue the opposite. Sometimes, having less information can be better. Reading less information about a business, for many people, can make decision making more accurate.

Let's say, for example, that two people are shopping for groceries. Each person needs to purchase 50 food items for a party. However, there is a difference between their shopping methods. The first individual creates a shopping list before coming to the grocery store. The second person doesn't create a shopping list. Instead, the second person plans on walking through the entire store and picking up the items as they pass by them.

Who do you think is more likely to obtain all 50 items?

In all likelihood, the first person is more likely to leave the store with all 50 items. Every time they pick up an item, they are going to cross it off their list. Then, before checking out, they are going to check whether they have crossed out all the items. And if some items are left uncrossed, they know that they must grab more items before they leave.

On the other hand, the second person will likely overlook some of the items. Of course, they will pass by every item that they need. However, they may not notice every item because some items might not be at eye level, causing them to forget about them. Even if they see an item, they might not remember, in the moment, that they need it. Moreover, they won't be able to use a list to double check that they grabbed everything before checking out. Therefore, they would merely need to rely on memory and hope that they didn't forget anything important.

When investing, you want to be like the first person. You want to approach a potential investment with a shopping list (or rubric). If you have a list of the two to five most important factors in a business, you are unlikely to overlook any of them. On the other hand, you don't want to be like the second person. Without a rubric, you are likely to overlook important determinants of long-term business success and failure.

In fact, a 5-minute rubric is especially important when investing.

Commonly used information sources—annual reports, quarterly reports, earnings transcripts, and industry reports—often don't tell you everything you need to know about a company. Let's say that you were attempting to predict Apple's future when the iPhone was a new product. To do that accurately, you would have needed to understand the quality of Apple's iPhone relative to the competition. That would have involved learning about the iPhone's design, user interface, and features—the key determinants of consumers' preferences for one phone over another. However, such information wouldn't have been in commonly used information sources.

You wouldn't have found much information about the iPhone's user interface in an earnings transcript.

You wouldn't have learned how the iPhone's design compared to the competition by reading an annual report.

In fact, most industry reports wouldn't even have told you what to look for in a well-designed product.

Such information—which would have been highly important to making an investment—just didn't exist in commonly used information sources.

So, what would have happened if you had simply "researched the business thoroughly" like most people? You would have read through all the conventional information sources. You would have read the company's annual reports and earnings transcripts. But you wouldn't have come across information about the iPhone's design and user interface. As a result, you would have made an investment decision in Apple without looking at one of its most important determinants of success: the product.

Having a rubric, however, would have prevented that problem. With a rubric, you would have a list of the most important factors to consider. This is just like having a shopping list that contains the most important items to buy.

Then, while reading through conventional sources of information, you would have started to check off items as you came across them. For example, if low debt was an item on your rubric, you would have crossed that off as soon as you concluded that Apple had low debt, just as you would cross items off your shopping list as you put them in your cart.

Once you finished researching Apple, you would have been able to check whether everything was crossed off your rubric. In this case, you would have noticed that the iPhone's design wasn't covered in annual or quarterly reports, despite being on your rubric. You would have realized that you didn't have enough information yet to make an intelligent investment decision. So, you would have gone back to get that crucial piece of information. In the end, you would have avoided overlooking a critical piece of information. This is just like reviewing your shopping list before checking out to see if you got everything important.

In fact, having rubrics is good for making decisions in life in general. Several times throughout this book, I have pointed out that several companies launched marketing campaigns that were bound to fail. You may have been wondering, how could a college student claim that large, multi-billion-dollar companies were running advertising campaigns that were essentially bound to fail? How could he spot mistakes that experienced Chief Marketing Officers couldn't? The answer lies in the five-minute rubric. I had a 5-minute rubric of the most important criteria an ad needed to succeed. I saw that virtually all the ads of those companies didn't meet any of the criteria on my list. Hence, I concluded that they were bound to fail. I was right, and the Chief Marketing Officers were wrong.

Therefore, you always want to have a 5-minute rubric for making investment decisions. Not only does it facilitate efficient decision making, but also, it greatly reduces the chances of overlooking anything important and knowable.

On the surface, the lessons in this chapter seem hypocritical. The entire thesis of this chapter is that it is possible to make investment decisions quickly by forming rubrics. On the other hand, the thesis of The 80% Past Rule was that investors need to spend many hours reading books and old annual reports to make investment decisions. Therefore, it would appear that the lessons in each of the chapters directly contradict one another.

However, it is important to recognize an important subtlety between the lessons in each of those chapters. The 80% Past Rule was all about building your circle of competence. It was about identifying what needs to be on your rubric. On the other hand, this chapter was about making actual investment decisions. It was not about making your rubric, but actually using it.

Of course, learning about a business takes a lot of time. You must read many books and annual reports to understand what matters in a business. That even holds true for simple businesses like Coca-Cola. You have to read a lot to understand a simple business like Coca-Cola. In other words, it requires a lot of effort to form a sound rubric, especially if you want to take investing seriously.

But once you have your 5-minute rubric formed and know what to look for, it doesn't take much time to analyze a business. Once your 5-minute rubric is formed, you don't need to read every little detail about a company in an annual report. You just need to focus on what your 5-minute rubric says to focus on, which, in some cases, can allow you to make investment decisions in just a few minutes.

BACK TESTING YOUR RUBRIC

Several times throughout this book, we talked about Ray Dalio. To jog your memory, he was the macro investor who predicted that a great depression would come. He saw that Mexico defaulted on its debts, and he saw that many other countries had similar credit risks. Thus, he concluded that the other countries would default as well. But he was wrong because he underestimated the Fed's and the IMF's abilities to keep the economic situation stable. Since his prediction was so wrong, his reputation was ruined, cost[ing him] just about everything [he] had built at Bridgewater," and putting him "back to square one."

But as we know, Dalio is incredibly successful, and has a very good reputation today. So, what happened in between? How did he go from "square one" to his level of success today?

Well, one thing he started doing more closely afterwards was studying history. As mentioned earlier, "going back to square one" made him more cognizant of the importance of studying history:

> I again saw the value of studying history. What had happened, after all, was "another one of those." I should have realized that debts denominated in one's own currency can be successfully restructured with the government's help, and that when central banks simultaneously provide stimulus (as they did in March 1932, and the low point of the Great Depression, and as they did again in 1982), inflation and deflation can be balanced against each other. As in 1971, I had failed to recognize the lessons of history.

But what I haven't told you is that merely reading history wasn't all that Ray Dalio did to propel his success after that failure. He also did what I call back testing your rubric.

As mentioned earlier, many intelligent individuals—in one way or another—use rubrics to make investment decisions. Warren Buffett and Charlie Munger have filters that allow them to make investment decisions far faster than 99% of investors (and do a better job of it). Strategy consultants like Heinrich Rusche use frameworks to solve problems. Similarly, Ray Dalio had his decision-making criteria written down before he made a trade. As he wrote in his book *Principles*:

> From very early on, whenever I took a position in the markets, I wrote down the criteria I used to make my decision.

One of the major weaknesses associated with using rubrics, however, is that your 5-minute rubric might be wrong. In particular, the 5-minute rubric you create might be missing an important criterion to look for in a business.

In fact, that's an incredibly common problem among investors.

We saw this in the previous chapter when we talked about how most investors evaluate Tesla. We mentioned that most investors would evaluate Tesla by analyzing its products, its financials, and its management team, which aren't wrong to analyze. However, 90%+ of investors would overlook the importance of Tesla's culture to its success. The mental rubrics of those investors have, in a sense, neglected an importance investment criterion.

We saw this with Coca-Cola at the beginning of the book. When most investors analyze Coca-Cola, they think about factors such as product quality and financials. But they forget that the brand attempts to associate itself with happiness; they forget to analyze the reputation of the brand—the whole point of building a brand. Hence, the mental rubrics of those investors overlooked an important factor.

We saw this with Dalio as well. When Mexico defaulted on its debts, Dalio thought that a depression would ensue. However, his decision-making criteria overlooked a plausible scenario where the IMF and Fed would be able to keep the economy under control, causing him to ruin his short-term reputation.

One of the best ways to ensure that your 5-minute rubric doesn't omit anything major is by back testing your 5-minute rubric. What I mean is that you want to use history to understand the predictive accuracy of your 5-minute rubric.

For example, let's say that you are investing in an oil and gas company. One way that you could make the investment is by first creating a 5-minute rubric of the three to seven most important factors and then evaluating oil and gas companies against your 5-minute rubric. That wouldn't be wrong. But the risk you would be taking is that your 5-minute rubric is wrong, which could cause you to incorrectly evaluate a business.

Instead, you would want to back test that 5-minute rubric against history to see whether it is accurate at predicting whether a business will succeed or fail. To do so, you would want to read an old annual report of an oil and gas company. Once you read that old annual report, you would want to use your 5-minute rubric to predict what the company's competitive positioning, sales, and profits will look like over the next 10 years. Then, you would want to use recent annual reports to check whether you were right about your predictions.

If you were right, that's great. That means your 5-minute rubric has good predictive value.

If not, your 5-minute rubric was simply missing something important. In that case, recent annual reports would help you understand why your prediction was off. Reading them would allow you to understand what criterion your 5-minute rubric omitted, allowing you to refine it.

When you back test your 5-minute rubric once, it's simply a matter of repeating the process. Read another old annual report of a company in the same industry. Predict its future. Then check your answer and revise your 5-minute rubric. And then repeat the process again. Read another old annual report. Predict its future. Check your answer. Revise your 5-minute rubric. And repeat.

In fact, Dalio would follow a similar process when trying to improve the accuracy of his decision-making rules. As he explains in *Principles:*

> From very early on, whenever I took a position in the markets, I wrote down the criteria I used to make my decision. Then, when I closed out a trade, I could reflect on how well these criteria had worked. It occurred to me that if I wrote those criteria into formulas (now more fashionably called algorithms) and then ran historical data through them, I could test how well my rules would have worked in the past.... And [then] modify the decision rules appropriately.

Warren Buffett even learned how to value companies by back testing. Ben Graham, Buffett's teacher, would show him the financials of a couple of companies. Then, he would ask Buffett to estimate what those companies were worth. And finally, they would check their answer against recent financial figures to understand whether they were correct, and if they were incorrect, why. As Buffett once said:

> Well, I was lucky. I had a sensational teacher, Ben Graham.... Ben made it terribly interesting, because what we did was walk into that class and value companies. And he had various little games he would play with us. Sometimes he would have us evaluate company A and company B with a whole bunch of figures, and then we would find out that A and B were the same company at different points in its history, for example.... There were a lot of little games he played to get us to think about the key variables and how we could go off the track.

Therefore, before you implement a 5-minute rubric or set of filters to make investment decisions, back test. Ensure that your 5-minute rubric has a high level of predictive accuracy. That's really how Outlier Investors like Buffett learned how to invest in the first place, and it is how Outlier Investors like Ray Dalio prevent themselves from "going back to square one."

* *

Warren Buffett acquired FlightSafety in 5 minutes because thorough due diligence isn't what makes an investment successful.

* *

The Framework

· ·

Warren Buffett once said that investing does not require you to be smart, nor does it require you to have inside information. But it does require a sound framework for making decisions:

> To invest successfully over a lifetime does not require a stratospheric IQ, unusual business insights, or inside information. What's needed is a sound intellectual framework for making decisions and the ability to keep emotions from corroding that framework.

In the previous chapter, we really did talk about frameworks. I used the term rubrics, but those were really frameworks. According to one dictionary, a framework is simply "a particular set of rules, ideas, or beliefs which you use in order to deal with problems or to decide what to do." That's exactly what five-minute rubrics are: a set of rules or, as Ray Dalio would say, "decision- making criteria," that you can use to evaluate any business.

Now, I'm going to take that same concept and apply it to investing, more broadly. Based on the lessons throughout this book, I'm going to provide you with a high-level framework for approaching investment decisions. This is a set of instructions that illustrates how to make intelligent investment decisions. Before making any investment decision, you should read the following pages. Doing so will ensure that you are following a sound decision-making process.

STEP 1:
BUILD A CIRCLE OF COMPETENCE

Before you make any investment, the first question to ask yourself is, "can I create a five-minute rubric that lists the important second-layer drivers in the business and that doesn't list the second-layer drivers that aren't important." If you can't confidently do that, you don't know what's important to the success of the business. In other words, you don't understand the business. Even if that business is Coca-Cola or McDonald's, you don't understand it if you can't differentiate between what is important and what isn't.

If you don't understand a business, that's fine. That's, in fact, normal. You shouldn't expect to understand a business without devoting time to studying it. There are several methods for building your circle of competence:

- **Follow the 80% Past Rule:** Allocate a significant amount of time towards studying history. You want to develop an understanding of the second-layer drivers of why businesses succeed and fail. Moreover, you need to understand how those drivers can impact the financial success of a company. As Charlie Munger has said, "I would try to relate the changes in the [Value Line] graph... to what happened in the business."

- **Stress Test Business:** When you don't understand a risk, stress test the business. Look at times when that risk has occurred in the past. That will give you a sense of how resilient the company is to various stressors.

- **Acknowledge the problem of the annual report:** Companies fill their annual reports with what makes Wall Street happy. That's typically financial data. However, only understanding financial figures is not enough to make sound investment decisions. You must also understand qualitative factors that drive business success. With Coca-Cola, for example, you must understand what its brand is associated with. However, in many annual reports, you rarely find much qualitative information. One of Coca-Cola's recent annual reports, for example, devoted less than a quarter of a page to discussing its "promotional and marketing programs." Thus, it is valuable to broaden your research beyond annual reports and earnings transcripts and read information sources such as books and articles.

- **Read what's important, not what's relevant:** Sometimes, we read something merely because it sounds relevant. We like to read the annual reports of restaurants if we are investing in a restaurant. And we like to read the industry reports of software companies if we are investing in a software company. However, as previously explained, information that sounds relevant is not necessarily what's important; many irrelevant information sources can provide tremendous insight, while relevant information sources may not provide significant insight. Thus, whenever you are learning about a business, read something because you think it has a high probability of producing important insights, not because it sounds relevant.

- **Back test, back test, back test:** The purpose of building a circle of competence is to develop a five-minute rubric so that you can make decisions efficiently, effectively, and correctly. However, a 5-minute rubric is only helpful if it has predictive value. Therefore, you should repeatedly back test it until you feel comfortable with its ability to predict future business success.

STEP 2: PREDICT THE FUTURE COMPETITIVE POSITIONING OF THE COMPANY

Once you understand a business, the next step is to predict it. At the end of the day, investing is about being able to predict the future of a business. If you can't figure out where the business will be in five to ten years, you shouldn't expect to know where the stock will be in five to ten years. Thus, you need to be able to reasonably predict where a business will be in the future. To do so, follow these two pieces of advice:

- **Focus on what's knowable and important:** At the end of the day, you can't accurately predict the future of a company if too many important pieces of information aren't knowable. If you focus on too many things that are unimportant yet knowable, you'll bias your thinking and inaccurately predict a company's future. Thus, focus on what's both knowable and important.

- **Invest on First Principles:** Ideas can sound perfectly logical but be terribly illogical. Warren Buffett and Charlie Munger initially thought See's Candies was an extremely overvalued business. Within their context, that wasn't an illogical conclusion to make. But it was terribly wrong. Similarly, it was perfectly logical to say that cars wouldn't replace horses because grass would continue to be plentiful. But that was terribly wrong, too. To minimize the chance of making perfectly logical but terribly illogical conclusions, always invest on first principles. Always start with the fundamental (undeniable) truths about the way the world works. Then, reason up from there.

STEP 3:
EVALUATE REWARD

Investing is about giving up cash today for more cash in the future.

Think of stock market investing as the same thing as rental property investing.

When you buy a rental property, you are giving up cash today for more cash in the future. You are spending money to purchase a rental property. Then, you are collecting rent from tenants. However, all that rent is not your own. A portion must go towards expenses: utilities, water, and repairs. What is left over after expenses is your profit.

If you were investing in a rental property, you would want to maximize your return on investment. Let's say that there are two rental properties: A and B. Rental property A costs $100,000, and it can expect to produce about $10,000 in profit per year. Rental property B costs $200,000, and it will produce $40,000 in profit per year. Which one would you rather own? Rental property B for sure. Of course, it costs about $100,000 more, but its produces four times as much profit. In other words, the return on investment of property B is much higher. With rental property A, you only earn a 10% return on your investment every year ($10,000 divided by $100,000); you are getting 10% of your initial investment back every year. On the other hand, with rental property B, you are earning $40,000 back per year for initially investing $200,000, which works out to be a 20% return on investment per year ($40,000 divided by $200,000).

You want to think about evaluating businesses in the same way that you think about evaluating rental properties.

Like rental properties, businesses produce rent every year. But, in a business context, the term isn't called rent. It's called sales or revenues.

Like rental properties, businesses have expenses like gas, utilities, and water bills. But, on a company's income statement, expenses aren't referred to as gas, utilities, or repairs. Instead, they are called cost of goods sold (COGS) and selling, general, and administrative expenses (SG&A).

Like rental properties, businesses produce profits. For a business, profits are called free cash flow.[24]

Just as a rental property costs money to buy, a business costs money to buy. The term that measures the cost of a business is called "market capitalization," "market cap," or "valuation." It is the price of the business.[25]

When investing in rental properties, if all else is equal, you

---

24   There are many metrics investors use to measure a company's profitability: net income, EBITDA, EBIT, free cash flow, adjusted net income, adjusted earnings per share, adjusted EBITDA, and several more. Free cash flow is generally considered the best measure of a company's profitability. I won't dive deep into the reasons why. But the simple answer is that it closely tracks how much cash a company is producing. To calculate it, subtract a company's operating cash flow from its capital expenditures. Both figures can be found on a company's cash flow statement. Some websites will have this figure calculated for you. For example, as of today, Yahoo Finance does. Just search for a stock and click on the "Financials" tab. Then select "Cash Flow Statement." A company's free cash flow will then be shown on the bottom of the cash flow statement.

25   Finance professionals generally use "enterprise value" instead of "market capitalization" to measure the purchase price of a business. I recommend new investors use market capitalization. In my opinion, using market capitalization is simpler and, intuitively, makes more sense. Moreover, throughout this book, I use the term "free cash flow" loosely. There are several different ways free cash flow can be calculated. This book refers to the "free cash flow to equity holders" calculation of free cash flow.

always want to own the property that will provide the highest return on investment. The same is true for investing in businesses. You want to invest in businesses that will produce a higher return on investment.

Whenever you invest in a business, look at the market cap. Realize that is the price of the business. Then, based on back testing and conducting Steps 1 and 2, ask yourself two sets of questions.

First, "how much money do I think this business will make in the future? Roughly what sort of return on investment can I expect to make each year?"

Second, "will this business provide a higher return on investment than if I simply invested in another business? Could I wait a little longer to find a business that will earn a higher return on investment?"

Obviously, if you believe that a business will produce a higher return on investment than other opportunities, it is a good opportunity, assuming that it doesn't contain much risk. Conversely, if you think that a business won't provide an attractive return on investment, it simply isn't a good opportunity.

STEP 4:
EVALUATE RISK

Of course, merely buying the company that will provide the highest return on investment won't work. You also need to minimize risk.

- **Invest with a margin of safety:** It's always a sound idea to buy a stock with a margin of safety. If you think a stock will give a 6.5% return on investment while the average business of that kind provides a 6.0% return on investment, it wouldn't be a good idea to buy the stock that offers a 6.5% return on investment. Why? Although it offers a higher return on investment than other companies, it doesn't offer a significantly one. Hence, there isn't room for error or a margin of safety. In that case, some little thing might unexpectedly go wrong, preventing the investment from working out. Thus, invest with a margin of safety.

- **But not just a margin of safety:** However, it is important to recognize the limitations of a margin of safety. A margin of safety can't protect a business from tail risks. Warren Buffett likely purchased Dexter Shoe with a margin of safety, but it turned out poorly because a tail risk occurred. When investing, then, you want to look for a business that is insulated against all sorts of tail risks. Of course, you don't know how all tail risks might impact a company. What would happen to Apple's business if its headquarters caught on fire? How would Tesla fare during World War III? You can't really assess those risks. But what you can assess—and which are more important—are competitive tail risks: ones caused by competitors creating significantly better products, brands, and distribution capabilities. To assess them, conduct the billion-dollar test. Before buying any stock, ask yourself, "if I had a billion dollars, could I figure out any way to overthrow this business?" If you could think of a strategy that could overthrow the business, someone will probably execute it eventually. Someone may not execute it this year, next year, or even in the next five years. But they will likely execute it eventually. And you don't want to be owning the business when that tail risk occurs.

- **Deal with hidden risks:** It's important to recognize that many important risks can't be researched by merely reading annual reports, quarterly reports, and industry reports. Joe Campbell, who shorted KaloBios, could have read everything about the company, but none of those information sources would have told him anything about the risk of someone attempting to turn the company around. A mental tool that could help you uncover hidden risks is seeking to understand what assumptions need to hold true for your conclusions to hold true.

- **Know when you know enough, and when you don't:** One of the biggest mistakes when investing is overestimating how much you know. Coca-Cola was a vivid illustration of this. Everyone thinks they understand it, but very few people actually do. To become an Outlier Investor, you must know when you truly understand a business and when you really don't. To do so, you must be relentless about ensuring that you know everything important and knowable.

STEP 5:
MAXIMIZE REWARD, MINIMIZE RISK

Once you complete steps 1-4, you'll have a good sense of the risk-reward characteristics of the businesses. Then, you simply need to buy the stock that comes with the most reward and the least risk. And you're done. You've made a sound investment decision like an Outlier Investor.

Advice from Mao Ye

A finance professor of mine, Mao Ye, once said that there are four levels to learning finance. First, understand the finance concepts. Second, pass the test. Third, apply what you learn in college finance classes to improve your financial situation. Fourth, apply what you learn in college finance classes to life, more generally. Readers of this book will hit levels 1 and 3 (level 2 is irrelevant because I don't have a test for you). Most people will understand the concepts in this book, and many people will, hopefully, apply them to make intelligent investment decisions. However, as Mao Ye highlighted, most people have difficulty reaching the fourth level—applying finance concepts to improve other aspects of their lives. But in my view, it is a serious loss to not apply these concepts to life. If you apply them to life, you'll be able to do phenomenal things.

Several times throughout this book, I have pointed out that several companies launched marketing campaigns that were bound to fail. You may have been wondering, how could a college student claim that large, multi-billion-dollar companies were running advertising campaigns that were essentially bound to fail? How could he spot mistakes that experienced Chief Marketing Officers couldn't? The answer lies in the five-minute rubric. I had a 5-minute rubric of the most important criteria an ad needed to succeed. I saw that virtually all the ads of those companies didn't meet any of the criteria on my list. Hence, I concluded that they were bound to fail. I was right, and the Chief Marketing Officers were wrong.

Contact Information

· ·

LinkedIn:
Danial Jiwani

Email:
danial.jiwani@danialjiwani.com

A Note on Sources

All sources have been appropriately cited to the best of the author's knowledge. If any sources are believed to be omitted, please contact the author at danial.jiwani@danialjiwani.com. In some cases, however, sources were intentionally not cited. This only occurred if *Outlier Investors* talked about any companies in a negative way and if the author chose to keep those companies anonymous. For example, the introduction talks about several major actively managed funds that have underperformed, despite claiming to implement Warren Buffett's investment style. To protect the brand name of those funds, the author intentionally chose not to cite those companies.

THE PURPOSE OF THIS BOOK

About 85% of large-cap, actively managed funds underperformed the market over a 10 year period: Pisani, Bob. "Stock Picking Has a Terrible Track Record, and It's Getting Worse." *CNBC*, CNBC, 22 Sept. 2020, https://www.cnbc.com/2020/09/18/stock-picking-has-a-terrible-track-record-and-its-getting-worse.html.

From 1964-2021, Berkshire Hathaway had an overall gain of 3,641,613%, whereas the S&P 500 returned only 30,209%: BERKSHIRE HATHAWAY INC. www.berkshirehathaway.com/2021ar/2021ar.pdf.

Warren Buffett has said that he would be perfectly comfortable only owning three stocks in his portfolio: "Warren Buffett Explains How Many Stocks You Should Own in Your Portfolio." Www.youtube.com, www.youtube.com/watch?v=bHPzQIW_pww&t=179s. Accessed 13 Aug. 2022.

Peter Lynch, who ran Fidelity's Magellan Fund for 13 years. During that period, he earned 29.2% per year, more than twice the return of the S&P 500: Chen, James. "Peter Lynch." Investopedia, www.investopedia.com/terms/p/peterlynch.asp.

[Ted Welcher and Todd Combs] are both absolutely terrific: Buffett, Warren. "Warren Buffett on Todd Combs & Ted Weschler: 'I Don't Want People Quizzing Them on Stocks'." *YouTube*, YouTube, 3 May 2021, https://www.youtube.com/watch?v=9kaLV_ykRC0.

NO ONE UNDERSTANDS COCA-COLA

I'm a very opinionated man, and I know a lot: Munger, Charlie. "Charlie Munger on Apple Inc. | Daily Journal 2019." *YouTube*, YouTube, 6 Sept. 2020, https://www.youtube.com/watch?v=IWLMG1F7K08.

Peter Lynch, an Outlier Investor who returned over 29% per year for 13 years: Mohamed, Theron. "Legendary Investor Peter Lynch Breaks with Warren Buffett, Warning Passive Investors They're Losing Out and Backing the Best Fund Managers to Keep Beating the Market." *Business Insider*, Business Insider, 8 Dec. 2021, https://markets.businessinsider.com/news/stocks/peter-lynch-warren-buffett-passive-investing-index-funds-active-management-2021-12#:~:text=Lynch%20is%20best%20known%20for,managers'%20performance%20is%20easily%20measured

"Know what you own and know why you own it:" Jon. "Peter Lynch: The Single Most Important Thing • Novel Investor." Novel Investor, 26 Apr. 2017, novelinvestor.com/peter-lynch-single-important-thing/.

Do most GoPro products get used by athletes and scuba divers? Based on the number of cameras it sells, probably not. The fact that the media that follow Apple (Nasdaq: AAPL) would even make a comparison between an iPhone 6s and a GoPro Hero 4 is damaging all by itself.... With the launch of the iPhone 7 just months away, the odds that it will marginalize GoPro products could destroy GoPro's appeal more than Apple already has: Apple's iPhone Ruins GoPro – 24/7 Wall St. 247wallst.com/consumer-electronics/2015/11/16/apples-iphone-ruins-gopro/. Accessed 18 Aug. 2022.

Never rely on market research: Smith, Dave. "What Everyone Gets Wrong about This Famous Steve Jobs Quote, according to Lyft's Design Boss." *Business Insider*, www.businessinsider.com/steve-jobs-quote-mis-understood-katie-dill-2019-4#:~:text=.

Less than half of the participants (45%) thought that the cup of Pepsi contained Pepsi. 39% thought it was Coca-Cola, while 16% thought it was another drink or just couldn't tell: Ramanjaneyalu, N. "Ijaiem." *Blind Taste Test of Soft-Drinks – A Comparison Study on Coke and Pepsi*, International Journal of Application or Innovation in Engineering & Management (IJAIEM), https://ijaiem.org/volume2issue12/IJAIEM-2013-12-26-071.pdf.

TNS Impulse Panel (UK) conducted a duplication of purchases analysis of the cola industry: Sharp, Byron, and Jenni Romaniuk. "Who Do You Really Compete With?" *How Brands Grow*, Oxford University Press, Melbourne, 2016, pp. 75–81.

According to one marketing agency, Coca-Cola's brand is "known for being positive, simple, and classic," whereas Pepsi's brand is perceived as being exciting, fresh, and young:" Sievers, Clarissa. "Pepsi or Coke? an in-Depth Look at Decades of Marketing Rivalry." *Pinckney Marketing*, 21 Apr. 2020, https://pinckneymarketing.com/coke-vs-pepsi-rivalry/.

World-class market researcher Byron Sharp wanted to understand whether buyers perceived their brand as being differentiated from the competition. So, he ran a study to get an answer: Sharp, Byron, and Jenni Romaniuk. "Differentiation Versus Distinctiveness ." *How Brands Grow*, Oxford University Press, Melbourne, 2016, pp. 123–125.

"We were buying a second-class department store at a third-class price:" Joe and Diversified Retailing. www.valueinvestingworld.com/2014/07/berkshire-and-diversified retailing.html. Accessed 13 Aug. 2022.

"Within the first couple of years at Hochschild-Kohn, Buffett had figured out that the essential skill in retailing was merchandising, not finance:" Joe and Diversified Retailing. www.valueinvestingworld.com/2014/07/berkshire-and-diversified retailing.html. Accessed 13 Aug. 2022.

"We didn't weigh heavily enough the intense competition between four different department stores in Baltimore at a time when department stores no longer had an automatic edge:" Joe and Diversified Retailing. www.valueinvestingworld.com/2014/07/berkshire-and-diversified retailing.html. Accessed 13 Aug. 2022.

So, within three years of buying Hochschild-Kohn, they sold it. Luck-

ily, however, they were able to get their initial capital back by selling it: "Mohnish Pabrai on Diversified Retailing " Buffett's Investment That on Body Talks About"." Www.youtube.com, www.youtube.com/watch?v=SQUB92Zvufk.

"Charlie and I have been reasonably good at identifying what I would call the perimeter of my circle of competence. But obviously, we have gone out of it. In my own case...store in Baltimore [Hochschild-Kohn]:" "Warren Buffett - How to Know Your Circle of Competence." Www.youtube.com, www.youtube.com/watch?v=ii8tDwkizJQ. Accessed 13 Aug. 2022.

The first glass of Coca-Cola was sold in 1886: "Coca-Cola History." *The Coca-Cola Company*, https://www.coca-colacompany.com/company/history.

Whereas Pepsi was merely founded in 1965: "About Pepsico." *PepsicoUpgrade*, https://www.pepsico.com/who-we-are/about-pepsico.

Warren Buffett, Charlie Munger, and Sandy Gottesman, a current board member of Berkshire Hathaway, created a holding company called Diversified Retailing. Buffett owned 80%, Munger owned 10%, and Gottesman owned 10%: "Mohnish Pabrai on Diversified Retailing " Buffett's Investment That Nobody Talks About"." Www.youtube.com, www.youtube.com/watch?v=SQUB92Zvufk. Accessed 13 Aug. 2022.

That gave Coca-Cola over 50 years to establish its brand as the drink that "makes [people] smile," allowing Coca-Cola to assert itself without significant competition: "Coca-Cola Study Measures Global Happiness; Study Reveals Human Contact Brings Most Happiness in an Increasingly Digital World." *The Coca-Cola Company*, 11 May 2010, https://investors.coca-colacompany.com/news-events/press-releases/detail/26/coca-cola-study-measures-global-happiness-study-reveals.

Whereas Coca-Cola mainly operates in the beverage industry: "Brands & Products." *The Coca-Cola Company*, https://www.coca-colacompany.com/brands.

PepsiCo is more diversified into other areas. Most notably, it owns Frito Lay and Quaker Oats: "Our Products." *PepsicoUpgrade*, https://www.pepsico.com/our-brands/creating-smiles/our-products.

Coca-Cola has spent roughly $4 billion per year in advertising: *Coca-Cola Income Statement*, Capital IQ, https://www.capitaliq.com/CIQDotNet/Financial/IncomeStatement.aspx?CompanyId=26642. Accessed 5 Aug. 2022.

PepsiCo has spent roughly $5 billion per year in advertising: *PepsiCo Income Statement,* Capital IQ, https://www.capitaliq.com/CIQDotNet/Financial/IncomeStatement.aspx?CompanyId=32854. Accessed 5 Aug. 2022.

Coca-Cola will sell a billion and a half eight-ounce servings of its product around the world today: Buffett, Warren. "Everything Warren Buffett & Charlie Munger of Berkshire Hathaway Ever Said on Coke Coca-Cola & Pepsi." YouTube, 4 Oct. 2021, https://www.youtube.com/watch?v=wZ2kNIcahbw.

All of a sudden, we go from trying to get $10,000 to go do a shoot to somebody saying, 'Well, how about $100,000?' The company invested a massive amount: Foster, Tom. "The Untold Story of How Massive Success Made GoPro's CEO Lose His Way. Can He Recover?" *Inc.com,* Inc., 13 Dec. 2017, https://www.inc.com/magazine/201802/tom-foster/gopro-camera-drone-challenges.html.

"The first thing I must decide when somebody calls me is within my circle of competence... I mean understand what the economic characteristics of the business are and what the company is really going to look like in 5 or 10 or 20 years:" Warren Buffett | Lecture | University of Nebraska | 2003." Www.youtube.com, www.youtube.com/watch?v=N1t-3pVjvRjc&t=3746s. Accessed 13 Aug. 2022.

We went from being thrifty and scrappy and efficient and wildly innovative to being bloated and--what's the opposite of thrifty? It was undermining the strength of our brand and deconstructing everything we had built: Foster, Tom. "The Untold Story of How Massive Success Made GoPro's CEO Lose His Way. Can He Recover?" *Inc.com,* Inc., 13 Dec. 2017, https://www.inc.com/magazine/201802/tom-foster/gopro-camera-drone-challenges.html.

If you go to McDonald's, you cannot get a Pepsi. They only sell Coca-Cola. If you go to Subway, you cannot get a Pepsi. They only sell Coca-Cola. If you go to Burger King, you cannot get a Pepsi. They only sell Coca-Cola: Gould, Skye. "See Which Major US Restaurants Serve Coke vs. Pepsi." *Business Insider,* Business Insider, 3 Apr. 2017, https://www.businessinsider.com/which-restaurants-serve-coke-or-pepsi-2017-3.

And in 2009, Warren Buffett ended up selling over half of his ConocoPhillips stake at a loss: Berkshire Hathaway Inc. Form 10-K, https://www.berkshirehathaway.com/2009ar/2009ar.pdf.

Without urging from Charlie or anyone else, I bought a large amount of ConocoPhillips stock when oil and gas prices were near their peak:

Berkshire Hathaway Inc. Form 10-K, https://www.berkshirehathaway. com/2008ar/2008ar.pdf.

Nick noticed that Amazon benefited from a concept known as shared economies of scale. It said that Amazon's competitive advantage and sales would grow like a self-fulfilling cycle: Chua, Thomas. "Lessons from Nick Sleep of Nomad Investment Partnership." *Steady Compounding*, 31 Mar. 2022, https://steadycompounding. com/investing/sleep/.

Over the 13 years his investment fund was open, he delivered 921.1% returns, compared to 116.9% of the MSCI World Index: "Lessons from Nick Sleep of Nomad Investment Partnership." *Steady Compounding*, 31 Mar. 2022, https://steadycompounding.com/investing/sleep/.

Now, virtually every person in the globe—maybe, well, let's get it down to 75% of the people in the globe—have some notion in their mind about Coca-Cola: *Warren Buffett & Charlie Munger talk "the mind of the consumer."* (n.d.). Www.youtube.com. Retrieved August 5, 2022, from https://www.youtube.com/watch?v=ZI9ZBIL_Uew&t=206s

"I skate to where the puck is going to be, not to where it has been:" Canadian Business – Your Source For Business News. (2014, October 3). *CEOs: stop quoting Wayne Gretzky's "where the puck is going" quote.* Canadian Business. https://archive.canadianbusiness.com/blogs-and-comment/stop-using-gretzky-where-the-puck-is-quote/

FOLLOW THE 80% PAST RULE

One evening, Charlie Munger and Mohnish Pabrai were having dinner together: "Mohnish Pabrai: What Successful Value Investors Read? | UCI 2016(C:M.P Ep.116)." *Www.youtube.com*, www.youtube. com/watch?v=xC_ylmu7wfg&t=299s.

"If I were teaching in a business school, I would have value-line-type figures that took people through the entire history of General Motors. And I would try to relate the changes in the graph and in the data to what happened in the business": "How Charlie Munger Would Teach a Business School Course." Www.youtube.com, www. youtube.com/watch?v=TwSPttRiaok. Accessed 13 Aug. 2022.

Charlie Munger wanted to "just [get] better at knowing how the world works:" What Successful Value Investors Read? |

UCI 2016(C:M.P Ep.116)." *Www.youtube.com*, www.youtube.com/watch?v=xC_ylmu7wfg&t=299s.

"A lot of companies, for example, have investor relations people, and they are dying just to pump out what they think is good news all the time:" "Warren Buffett: Important & Not Important in Annual Reports." Www.youtube.com, www.youtube.com/watch?v=3SkDjI72z6A&t=135s. Accessed 13 Aug. 2022.

I again saw the value of studying history: Dalio, Ray. "My Abyss." *Principles: Life and Work*. Simon & Schuster, 2017, pp. 32-35.

For example, there were many sound reasons to invest in Blockbuster during the early 2000s: Antioco, John. "How I Did It: Blockbuster's Former CEO on Sparring with an Activist Shareholder." *Harvard Business Review*, Apr. 2011, hbr.org/2011/04/how-i-did-it-blockbusters-former-ceo-on-sparring-with-an-activist-shareholder.

Sales growth was strong. Between 1999 and 2003, sales grew from $4.4 billion to $5.9 billion: SECURITIES and EXCHANGE COMMISSION FORM 10-K Annual Report pursuant to Section 13 and 15(D). pdf. secdatabase.com/1077/0000930661-02-000951.pdf.

"I like to study failure actually...We want to see what has caused businesses to go bad:" Warren Buffett on Why He'll Never Sell a Share of Coke Stock - YouTube." *Www.youtube.com*, www.youtube.com/watch?v=4p1_5bZ8I4M.

Jeff Bezos' 2019 Letter to Shareholders is more about current initiatives in Amazon, such as their Diversity, Equity, and Inclusion initiatives and ESG initiatives: Amazon Inc., Jeff Bezos' 2019 Letter to Shareholders, https://s2.q4cdn.com/299287126/files/doc_financials/2020/ar/2019-Shareholder-Letter.pdf.

Moreover, Andy Jassy, the new CEO of Amazon, mainly talks more about financial KPIs and recent social initiatives in his 2021 Letter to Shareholders: Amazon Inc., Any Jassay's 2021 Letter to Shareholders, https://s2.q4cdn.com/299287126/files/doc_financials/2022/ar/2021-Shareholder-Letter.pdf

Accordingly, in that letter, Jeff Bezos talks about the most important reasons why Amazon is successful: Amazon Inc., Any Jassay's 2021 Letter to Shareholders, https://s2.q4cdn.com/299287126/files/doc_financials/2022/ar/2021-Shareholder-Letter.pdf

THE PROBLEM OF THE ANNUAL REPORT

· ·

"does not affect ongoing [buying] propensity and does not have favorable long-term effects:" Sharp, Byron, and Jenni Romaniuk. "What Price Promotions Really Do." *How Brands Grow*, Oxford University Press, Melbourne, 2016, pp. 167.

What they found is that brand campaigns were more effective at increasing brand salience than market share: Binet, Les, and Peter Field. *The Long and the Short of It: Balancing Short and Long-Term Marketing Strategies*. Institute Of Practitioners in Advertising, 2013. pp. 28-29.

I found that my language with our investors wasn't resonating because I spoke the customer's language: Dewar, Carolyn. *CEO EXCELLENCE : The Six Mindsets That Distinguish the Best Leaders from the Rest*. Scribner, 2022. pp. 266-267.

"[My] day job is reading, and I spend the vast majority of my day reading. I try to make half of that reading random things like newspapers and trade periodicals:" Todd Combs and Ted Weschler describe working for Berkshire Hathaway. (n.d.). Www.youtube.com. Retrieved August 5, 2022, from https://www.youtube.com/watch?v=aAmRTiYZNpM&t=3s

"I just read and read and read. I probably read 5-6 hours a day... I read five daily newspapers. I read a fair number of magazines. I read 10-K's. I read annual reports, and I read a lot of other things, too... I love reading biographies, for example": "Warren Buffett: I Read 5-6 Hours a Day | January 26, 2015." *Www.youtube.com*, www.youtube.com/watch?v=L-NmeADMxTuQ. Accessed 5 Aug. 2022.

First, as expected, he read Bank of America's annual report: "I probably read [Bank of America's] annual report every year for 50 years." Second, he said that he previously read a book called *Biography of a Bank: A rare interview with Ted Weschler, Todd Combs, Warren Buffett & Tracy Britt Cool* (2014). (n.d.). Www.youtube.com. Retrieved August 5, 2022, from https://www.youtube.com/watch?v=XvcSVCOroQ4&t=435s.

"Your personal experiences with money make up maybe 0.00000001% of what's happened in the world, but maybe 80% of how you think the world works:" Housel, Morgan. *The Psychology of Money: Timeless Lessons on Wealth, Greed, and Happiness*. Harriman House, 2020.

"I get in [to the office at] around seven or eight, and I read until about seven or eight at night. And I go home and see my family, and then I'll read for another hour or two in bed at night:" "Todd Combs and Ted Weschler Describe Working for Berkshire Hathaway." *Www.youtube.com*, www.youtube.com/watch?v=aAmRTiYZNpM&t=3s.

The former Chief Design Officer of Apple, Jony Ive, frequently looks to Dieter Rams' work for inspiration: "Dieter Rams Has a New Challenge for Apple | Cult of Mac." *Www.cultofmac.com*, www.cultofmac.com/581644/dieter-rams-documentary/. Accessed 5 Aug. 2022.

Dieter Rams said that "good design is as little design as possible:" "Dieter Rams' 10 Principles of Good Design - Heurio." *Www.heurio.co*, www.heurio.co/dieter-rams-10-principles-of-good-design.

Dieter Rams said that "good design is innovative:" "Dieter Rams' 10 Principles of Good Design - Heurio." *Www.heurio.co*, www.heurio.co/dieter-rams-10-principles-of-good-design.

Dieter Rams said that "good design makes a product understandable:" "Dieter Rams' 10 Principles of Good Design - Heurio." *Www.heurio.co*, www.heurio.co/dieter-rams-10-principles-of-good-design.

He made things like "clocks, radios, [and] calculators:" CNN, Jacopo Prisco. "Dieter Rams: The Legendary Designer Who Influenced Apple." *CNN*, www.cnn.com/style/article/dieter-rams-film-exhibition-style-intl/index.html. Accessed 5 Aug. 2022.

NOT JUST A MARGIN OF SAFETY

Which meant that Mutual Benefit had a "superior ability to meet their ongoing insurance obligations:" "AM Best Rating Scale." *Www.atlas-Mag.net*, www.atlas-mag.net/en/article/am-best-rating-scale.

A little before July 1991, several other insurance companies collapsed due to poor investments in junk bonds: Bates, et al. "First Capital Life Seized as Parent Firm Is Pressed: Insurance: The Second-Largest Failure of a Life Insurer Was Precipitated by Lenders' Attempt to Force Its Holding Company into Chapter 11." Los Angeles Times, 15 May 1991, www.latimes.com/archives/la-xpm-1991-05-15-fi-1781-story.html.

Mutual Benefit "was seen as a conservative, blue-chip company" that acquired over $13.8 billion in assets, making it the nation's 18th largest life insurance company: Zonana, et al. "Mutual Benefit Insurance Fails after Run on Assets: Economy: It Is the Largest Such Collapse in U.S. The New Jersey Company Cites Bad Real Estate Investments." *Los*

Angeles Times, 16 July 1991, www.latimes.com/archives/la-xpm-1991-07-16-mn-2351-story.html#:~:text=Until%2011%20days%20ago%2C%20Mutual.

On July 16th, 1991, the *Los Angeles Times* published an article with the following headline: "Mutual Benefit Insurance Fails After Run on Assets: It is the largest such collapse in U.S." By July 16th, the company lost its A+ rating and asked the New Jersey Department to help mitigate the financial consequences of the collapse: Zonana, et al. "Mutual Benefit Insurance Fails after Run on Assets: Economy: It Is the Largest Such Collapse in U.S. The New Jersey Company Cites Bad Real Estate Investments." *Los Angeles Times*, 16 July 1991, www.latimes.com/archives/la-xpm-1991-07-16-mn-2351-story.html#:~:text=Until%2011%20days%20ago%2C%20Mutual.

The insurance industry had to pay about $41.1 billion to customers for damages caused by Hurricane Katrina: Hartwig, Robert. *HURRICANE KATRINA: THE FIVE-YEAR ANNIVERSARY.* 2010, www.iii.org/sites/default/files/1007Katrina5Anniversary.pdf.

These were also fairly large names, such as Executive Life and First Capital. Seeing large insurance companies collapse spread fear: Becker, Murray, et al. "Session 61PD Insurance Company Failures of the Early 1990s-Have We Learned Anything?" *RECORD*, vol. 25, no. 1, 1999, www.soa.org/globalassets/assets/library/proceedings/record-of-the-society-of-actuaries/1990-99/1999/january/rsa99v25n161pd.pdf.

"There was almost a total lack of liquidity:" Becker, Murray, et al. "Session 61PD Insurance Company Failures of the Early 1990s-Have We Learned Anything?" *RECORD*, vol. 25, no. 1, 1999, www.soa.org/globalassets/assets/library/proceedings/record-of-the-society-of-actuaries/1990-99/1999/january/rsa99v25n161pd.pdf.

They have pledged to keep a minimum cash balance of $30 billion: Stempel, Jonathan. "Buffett Laments Lack of Good Investments Even as Berkshire Profit Sets Record." Reuters, 26 Feb. 2022, www.reuters.com/business/buffett-laments-lack-good-investments-even-berkshire-profit-sets-record-2022-02-26/.

A mini "stunt" Warren Buffett made during a Berkshire Hathaway meeting illustrates this. He pulled up a list of the 20 largest companies in the world measured by market cap: "TIMESAVER EDIT 2021 Berkshire Hathaway Annual Meeting Full Q&A with Warren Buffett & Charlie Munger." www.youtube.com/watch?v=npRYd31diFo. Accessed 13 Aug. 2022.

During a recent Berkshire Hathaway annual meeting, Warren Buffett noted that three of the largest reinsurance companies "came close to

extinction in the last 30 years" due to highly improbable, yet highly impactful risks. Two of those three companies even needed to make a deal with Berkshire Hathaway to help avoid extinction: "Morning Session – 2019 Berkshire Hathaway Annual Meeting." *Buffett.cnbc.com*, 4 May 2019, buffett.cnbc.com/video/2019/05/06/morning-session---2019-berkshire-hathaway-annual-meeting.html.

When I say that he was successful, I mean really successful. He never attended college, yet he managed to become the general manager of the trading division by the age of 28: "Who Is Nick Leeson?" *Investopedia*, www.investopedia.com/terms/n/nick-leeson.asp#:~:text=Nick%20Leeson%20was%20a%20orising. Accessed 5 Aug. 2022.

Reports state that he was so successful at trading derivatives that he once accounted for over 10% of the entire bank's profits: Smith, Elliot. "The Barings Collapse 25 Years On: What the Industry Learned after One Man Broke a Bank." *CNBC*, 26 Feb. 2020, www.cnbc.com/2020/02/26/barings-collapse-25-years-on-what-the-industry-learned-after-one-man-broke-a-bank.html.

But Nick Leeson chose not to report his losses: "Who Is Nick Leeson?" *Investopedia*, www.investopedia.com/terms/n/nick-leeson.asp#:~:text=Nick%20Leeson%20was%20a%20orising. Accessed 5 Aug. 2022.

The "secret account:" "Who Is Nick Leeson?" *Investopedia*, www.investopedia.com/terms/n/nick-leeson.asp#:~:text=Nick%20Leeson%20was%20a%20orising. Accessed 5 Aug. 2022.

On the 16th of January, 1995, Nick Leeson decided to initiate a short straddle on the Nikkei: "Who Is Nick Leeson?" *Investopedia*, www.investopedia.com/terms/n/nick-leeson.asp#:~:text=Nick%20Leeson%20was%20a%20orising. Accessed 5 Aug. 2022.

On the 17th of January, 1995, a major earthquake hit Japan: "Who Is Nick Leeson?" *Investopedia*, www.investopedia.com/terms/n/nick-leeson.asp#:~:text=Nick%20Leeson%20was%20a%20orising. Accessed 5 Aug. 2022.

Before leaving, however, he left Barings Bank a note to say "sorry" for losing $1.4 billion: "Who Is Nick Leeson?" *Investopedia*, www.investopedia.com/terms/n/nick-leeson.asp#:~:text=Nick%20Leeson%20was%20a%20orising. Accessed 5 Aug. 2022.

Dexter, I can assure you, needs no fixing: It is one of the best-managed companies Charlie [Munger] and I have seen in our business lifetimes: GmbH. "Warren Buffett's 'Most Gruesome Mistake' Was Buying Dexter Shoe. Here's the Story of His $9 Billion Error." *Markets.busines-sinsider.com*, markets.businessinsider.com/news/stocks/warren-buffett-most-gruesome-mistake-dexter-shoe-9-billion-error-2020-1-1028827359.

You've likely heard of the investing duo of Warren Buffett and Charlie Munger.... He sold his Berkshire stock to Warren—Warren actually said "I bought Rick's Berkshire stock"—at under $40 a piece. Rick was forced to sell because he was levered: Housel, Morgan. *The Psychology of Money: Timeless Lessons on Wealth, Greed, and Happiness*. Harriman House, 2020.

Or what about JCPenney? JCPenney was an iconic American business. In 1977, it was doing $10 billion in sales every year. In 1994, magazine *Women's Wear Daily* called JCPenney the "Number One Best Store For Women's Apparel.": Lisicky, Michael. "From Its Beginnings to Bankruptcy, a Historical Timeline of JCPenney." *Forbes*, www.forbes.com/sites/michaellisicky/2020/05/17/from-its-beginnings-to-bankruptcy--a-company-timeline-of--jcpenney/?sh=1763a44b31de.

There were very few companies that benefited from network effects more than MySpace. From 2004 to 2009, it was the world's largest social networking site. In 2006, it was visited more often than Google: Pugh, A. (2018, April). *10 businesses that failed to adapt*. Www.e-Careers.com. https://www.e-careers.com/connected/10-businesses-that-failed-to-adapt

In the 1970s, that company had dominated the footwear market. They had the most popular brand in the country. And they weren't the leading brand for one or two years, but for 20 years: *Six Takeaways From Phil Knight's Memoir*. (n.d.). Willamette Week. Retrieved August 5, 2022, from https://www.wweek.com/arts/2016/05/03/six-takeaways-from-phil-knights-memoir/

A brand like Nike, which was created in 1971: "Nike Company Profile." *Fortune*, fortune.com/company/nike/#:~:text=Founded%20in%20 1964%20as%20Blue.

They developed a better product and brand. And, by 1980, Nike had gained more market share than Adidas: Bain, Marc, and Shelly Banjo. "How Phil Knight Turned the Nike Brand into a Global Powerhouse." *Quartz*, Quartz, July 2015, qz.com/442042/more-than-anyone-else-it-was-phil-knight-who-built-nike-from-scratch-into-the-worlds-biggest-sports-brand/.

When Nike came along, Adidas was manufacturing its shoes in Europe: Willigan, Geraldine E. "High-Performance Marketing: An Interview with

Nike's Phil Knight." *Harvard Business Review*, Aug. 2014, hbr.org/1992/07/high-performance-marketing-an-interview-with-nikes-phil-knight.

Phil Knight even said in an interview that adding that cushion was "the first major breakthrough in running shoes in 50 years:" "Nike's Co-Founder on Innovation, Culture, and Succession." *Harvard Business Review*, 13 July 2017, hbr.org/podcast/2017/07/nikes-co-founder-on-inno-vation-culture-and-succession.

Every time I buy a business, I say to myself, 'If I had a billion dollars and [if] I wanted to go and compete with these guys, could I knock them off:' "The Most Eye Opening 70 Minutes of Your Life — Warren Buffett's Legendary Speech." *Www.youtube.com*, www.youtube.com/watch?v=9x8Z1M-B9IA&t=3407s. Accessed 5 Aug. 2022.

FIND HIDDEN RISKS

In 1973, it had over 2,000 locations: "In Pictures: The History of JCPenney." *CNN*, www.cnn.com/2020/05/19/us/gallery/jcpenney-history/index.html.

And it was doing over $6.2 billion in sales: "J.C. Penney Company Annual Reports: 1917–1960, 1962–1982, 1985–2004, 2006–2008, 2010." *Internet Archive*, archive.org/details/jcpenneyannualreports/jcpenney1973/page/n19/mode/2up. Accessed 5 Aug. 2022.

The company would attract customers by heavily discounting its merchandise. For example, they would initially price an item at $40. But it wouldn't sell any at that price. So, they would cut the price to $20 the following week. But it still wouldn't sell. So, they would send the customer some $10 coupons and provide some other discounts. And only then customers would start buying: "Bill Ackman: The Failed Investment of JCPenney." *Www.youtube.com*, www.youtube.com/watch?v=2C2Z75X6_g4. Accessed 5 Aug. 2022.

McDonald's generates about $600 in sales per square foot: Beyers, Tim. "McDonald's vs. Chipotle: Can You Guess Which Is the Better Business?" *The Motley Fool*, 26 Oct. 2014, www.fool.com/investing/general/2014/10/26/mcdonalds-vs-chipotle-can-you-guess-which-is-the-b.aspx#:~:text=According%20to%20most%20reports%20I.

He started his first hedge fund right after getting an MBA from Harvard Business School, and he grew assets under management from $3 million to $300 million dollars. Though his first hedge fund had to

close after a decade due to a poor investment, he later started a second hedge fund: Pershing Capital Management: "The Life and Career of Bill Ackman - the Hedge Fund Manager Everyone's Picking on These Days." *Business Insider*, www.businessinsider.in/finance/hedge-funds/the-life-and-career-of-bill-ackman-the-hedge-fund-manager-everyones-picking-on-these-days/slidelist/21603940.cms. Accessed 6 Aug. 2022.

Bill Ackman thought that Canadian Pacific "was the worst-run railroad in North America:" "Bill Ackman: The Failed Investment of JCPenney." *Www.youtube.com*, www.youtube.com/watch?v=2C2Z75X6_g4. Accessed 5 Aug. 2022.

However, he noticed that the business could be fixed with one simple solution. Just replace the "worst CEO in the railroad industry with the best CEO in the railroad industry." So, that's what he did. He acquired a 14% stake in Canadian Pacific, and he got one of the best railroad CEOs to run Canadian Pacific. After 16 months, Canadian Pacific became one of the most profitable railroads in North America, and the company's stock more than tripled: "Bill Ackman: The Failed Investment of JCPenney." *Www.youtube.com*, www.youtube.com/watch?v=2C2Z75X6_g4. Accessed 5 Aug. 2022.

Recognizing the opportunity, he quickly executed it. Bill Ackman bought a 16% stake in JCPenney and joined the board of directors: "Bill Ackman: The Failed Investment of JCPenney." *Www.youtube.com*, www.youtube.com/watch?v=2C2Z75X6_g4. Accessed 5 Aug. 2022.

One of Ron Johnson's turnaround initiatives was to implement a "fair and square pricing strategy:" "Bill Ackman: The Failed Investment of JCPenney." *Www.youtube.com*, www.youtube.com/watch?v=2C2Z75X6_g4. Accessed 5 Aug. 2022.

So, Ron Johnson came up with a brilliant solution. He suggested that JCPenney shouldn't initially sell items at high prices and then mark them down 2-3 times: "Bill Ackman: The Failed Investment of JCPenney." *Www.youtube.com*, www.youtube.com/watch?v=2C2Z75X6_g4. Accessed 5 Aug. 2022.

"The consumer knows the fair price" of all the items: "Bill Ackman: The Failed Investment of JCPenney." *Www.youtube.com*, www.youtube.com/watch?v=2C2Z75X6_g4. Accessed 5 Aug. 2022.

The results were phenomenal—phenomenally poor: "Bill Ackman: The Failed Investment of JCPenney." *Www.youtube.com*, www.youtube.com/watch?v=2C2Z75X6_g4. Accessed 5 Aug. 2022.

Sales fell from $17.2 billion in 2011 to $12.9 billion in 2012. JCPenney went from losing $150 million: JCPenney Form 10-K, pp. 51. https://www.annualreports.com/HostedData/AnnualReportArchive/j/NYSE_JCP_2012.pdf

Some media outlets refer to him as the man who "killed" JCPenney: Ladd, Brittain. "Ron Johnson Killed J.C. Penney—but He Has Become One of the Brightest Minds in Retail." *Observer*, 10 June 2019, observer.com/2019/06/ron-johnscon-jc-penney-retail-guru/.

Joe Campbell, your average Joe, initiated a $37,000 short position in KaloBios. (A short position is a bet that the stock will go down). KaloBios was a failed pharmaceutical company. At the time, KaloBios announced that it would shut down operations due to running out of cash. Moreover, they had hired a restructuring firm, Brenner Group, to liquidate the company: Langlois, Shawn. "Help! My Short Position Got Crushed, and Now I Owe E-Trade $106,445.56." *MarketWatch*, www.marketwatch.com/story/help-my-short-position-got-crushed-and-now-i-owe-e-trade-10644556-2015-11-19.

A frequently cited statistic that illustrates this point. In the 1960s, a researcher surveyed two groups of motorists: one group of motorists who had just crashed their cars and another group of motorists who had "an excellent driving record:" Farmer, On Behalf of, et al. "Studies Show Drivers Are Often Overconfident | Farmer, Cline & Campbell, PLLC | Farmer, Cline & Campbell, PLLC." *Www.farmerclinecampbell.com*, 24 Sept. 2018, www.farmerclinecampbell.com/blog/2018/09/studies-show-drivers-are-often-overconfident/#:~:text=However%2C%20another%20U.S.%20study%20found.

"expert" to "very poor:" Austad, Steven. "You Think You're a Pretty Good Driver, Don't You?" *Al*, 15 Sept. 2018, www.al.com/living/2018/09/you_think_youre_a_pretty_good.html.

Martin Shkreli, a hedge fund manager, thought that he could turn the company around. So, he acquired more than 50% of the outstanding shares. Consequently, the stock price went up 800%: "How a Short Seller's Account Went to Negative $106K (KBIO, ETFC)." *Investopedia*, www.investopedia.com/articles/investing/121515/how-short-sellers-account-went-negative-106k.asp. Accessed 6 Aug. 2022.

On top of that, he owed his brokerage over $100,000: "How a Short Seller's Account Went to Negative $106K (KBIO, ETFC)." *Investopedia*, www.investopedia.com/articles/investing/121515/how-short-sellers-account-went-negative-106k.asp. Accessed 6 Aug. 2022.

In pricing property coverages, for example, we had looked to the past and taken into account only costs we might expect to incur from windstorms, fires, explosions and earthquakes.... In short, all of us in the industry made a fundamental underwriting mistake by focusing on experience, rather than exposure, thereby assuming a huge terrorism risk for which we received no premium: Berkshire Hathaway Inc. Form 10-K. pp. 8. https://www.berkshirehathaway.com/2001ar/2001ar.pdf

Or take Ken Griffin as an example. Ken Griffin is the founder and CEO of Citadel, a successful hedge fund that manages $43 billion in assets: "Bloomberg - Are You a Robot?" *Www.bloomberg.com*, www.bloomberg.com/billionaires/profiles/kenneth-c-griffin/.

Ken Griffin himself has a net worth of $26 billion as of the time that I'm writing this, making him one of the richest people in the world: "Ken Griffin." *Forbes*, www.forbes.com/profile/ken-griffin/?sh=75ce13705079. Accessed 6 Aug. 2022.

The key to investing is not assessing how much an industry is going to affect society, or how much it will grow, but rather determining the competitive advantage of any given company and, above all, the durability of that advantage. The products or services that have wide, sustainable moats around them are the ones that deliver rewards to investors: "3 Things Investors Can Learn from Warren Buffett." *Www.morningstar.in*, www.morningstar.in/posts/64667/3-things-investors-can-learn-warren-buffett.aspx. Accessed 6 Aug. 2022.

Brexit forecasts hovered in the 50 percent range when most of his competitors thought the referendum had little chance of passing: Grant, A. (2021) "The Joy of Being Wrong," in *Think again: The power of knowing what you don't know*. New York, NY: Random House Large Print, pp. 65–67.

Jean-Pierre Beugoms has a favorite trick for catching himself when he's wrong: Grant, A. (2021) "The Joy of Being Wrong," in *Think again: The power of knowing what you don't know*. New York, NY: Random House Large Print, pp. 65–67.

KNOWN UNKNOWNS

One study found that employment in private equity backed companies decreases by almost 5% after they make an investment: Valladares, Mayra Rodriguez. "Private Equity Firms Have Caused Painful Job Losses and More Are Coming." *Forbes*, www.forbes.com/sites/mayrarodriguezvalladares/2019/10/30/private-equity-firms-have-caused-painful-job-losses-and-more-are-coming/?sh=4b54a6ca7bff. Accessed 6 Aug. 2022.

Buffett doesn't require them to tell him how much they plan on spending: "Here's How Warren Buffett Thinks about Berkshire's Incentive Comp Arrangements (1995 Q27 Pm)." *Www.youtube.com*, www.youtube.com/watch?v=m7VTNsjKfdE&t=148s. Accessed 6 Aug. 2022.

The CEO of one of our most successful subsidiaries, I may have talked to—unless I saw him here and just said hello—I've probably talked to him three times in the last 10 years. And he does remarkably well. He might have done even better if I hadn't talked to him those three times: Berkshire Hathaway. "Morning Session - 2018 Meeting." *CNBC*, CNBC, 5 May 2018, buffett.cnbc.com/video/2018/05/05/morning-session--2018-berkshire-hathaway-annual-meeting.html.

"height of foolishness:" Holodny, Elena. "Warren Buffett's Advice for CEOs Touches on a Key Issue Plaguing the US Economy." *Business Insider*, www.businessinsider.com/warren-buffett-rules-for-running-successful-company-2017-10#:~:text=Warren%20Buffett%2C%20generally%20speaking%2C%20likes. Accessed 6 Aug. 2022.

I feel like a horse's [expletive] for not identifying Google better... We screwed up... We could see in our own operations how well Google advertising was working. And we just sat there sucking our thumbs: "Morning Session - 2019 Berkshire Hathaway Annual Meeting." *Buffett.cnbc.com*, 4 May 2019, buffett.cnbc.com/video/2019/05/06/morning-session---2019-berkshire-hathaway-annual-meeting.html.

According to one source, about 20 million people visit the Disney Parks every year: *Walt Disney World Attendance by Day Is Going Up! - Disney Park Nerds*. 28 Feb. 2022, disneyparknerds.com/disney-world-attendance-by-day/.

While only 10 million people visit Hawaii every year: "Hawai'i Visitor Statistics Released for 2019." *Hawaii Tourism Authority*, 29 Jan. 2020, www.hawaiitourismauthority.org/news/news-releases/2020/hawai-i-visitor-statistics-released-for-2019/.

Disney's sales have consistently grown from 2000-2020: *Disney Income Statement*, Capital IQ, https://www.capitaliq.com/CIQDotNet/Financial/IncomeStatement.aspx?CompanyId=191564.

Risk managers mistakenly use hindsight as foresight.... Why then would anyone have expected a meltdown after that to be only as little as 23%? History fools many: "The Six Mistakes Executives Make in Risk

Management." *Harvard Business Review*, Aug. 2014, hbr.org/2009/10/the-six-mistakes-executives-make-in-risk-management.

We try to think about things that are important and things that are knowable.... And if you developed a view on these other subjects that in any way forestalled your acting on this, more specific, narrow view about the future of the company, you would have missed a great ride: "Warren Buffett Focuses on What Is Knowable and Important." *Www.youtube.com*, www.youtube.com/watch?v=kVrZHGr8HRQ. Accessed 6 Aug. 2022.

Herein lies the problem... the new euphemism for not earning a living: "Peter Lynch on the Challenges - GuruFocus.com." Www.gurufocus. com, www.gurufocus.com/news/1247298/peter-lynch-on-the-challenges-of-investing-in-biotech-stocks. Accessed 18 Aug. 2022.

Coca-Cola had lots of problems when it went public in 1919. Coca-Cola had "conflict[s] with the sugar industry and its bottlers," which caused the stock to go from $40 per share to $19 per share: The Story of The Coca-Cola Millionaires. (2015, October 17). *Void Magazine* | Jacksonville Florida | North Florida Culture. https://voidlive.com/the-story-of-the-coca-cola-millionaires/

INVEST ON FIRST PRINCIPLES

In fact, one time, the CEO of the business attempted to stop selling 14 of the company's products: "Why a Small Candy Company Is Warren Buffett's 'Dream' Investment." *Thehustleco*, thehustle.co/how-a-small-candy-company-became-warren-buffetts-dream-investment/. Accessed 6 Aug. 2022.

Since customers loved the products so much, they flooded the company with letters saying that the company must continue selling those products: "Why a Small Candy Company Is Warren Buffett's 'Dream' Investment." *Thehustleco*, thehustle.co/how-a-small-candy-company-became-warren-buffetts-dream-investment/. Accessed 6 Aug. 2022.

The business had cost roughly $25 million to buy, and it had $8 million in net tangible assets. So, the business was trading at slightly over three times its net tangible assets. In an ideal world, they would have wanted to pay less than $8 million for the business since it had $8 million in net tangible assets. So, this business was considered expensive by Warren Buffett and Charlie Munger since the owner was asking for $25 million for it: "Pricing a Box of Candy - Warre - GuruFocus.com." *Www.gurufocus.com*, www.gurufocus.com/news/229239/pricing-a-box-of-candy-warren-buffett-sees. Accessed 6 Aug. 2022.

You guys are all wrong on this. This is a wonderful company, and you're being way too chancy. There aren't many companies like this: "Charlie Munger: Barely Smart Enough to Buy See's Candies. | Redlands Forum 2020(C:C.M Ep.188)." *Www.youtube.com*, www.youtube.com/watch?v=agzTjIJZmzQ. Accessed 6 Aug. 2022.

Of course, Elon Musk can micromanage his direct reports. (And, according to some sources, he does micromanage them to a certain extent): Kolodny, Lora. "Elon Musk's Extreme Micromanagement Has Wasted Time and Money at Tesla, Insiders Say." CNBC, CNBC, 19 Oct. 2018, www.cnbc.com/2018/10/19/tesla-ceo-elon-musk-extreme-micro-manager.html.

There are some things [that] you should pay up for... You're underestimating quality: "Warren Buffett & Charlie Munger on See's Candy and Cigarbutt Approach V/S Buying Good Businesses." *Www.youtube.com*, www.youtube.com/watch?v=NwVMuC-IRD8. Accessed 6 Aug. 2022.

After hearing Ira Marshall's advice, Charlie Munger and Warren Buffett "listened to the criticism" of Ira Marshall: "Warren Buffett & Charlie Munger on See's Candy and Cigarbutt Approach V/S Buying Good Businesses." *Www.youtube.com*, www.youtube.com/watch?v=N-wVMuC-IRD8&t=2s. Accessed 6 Aug. 2022.

According to *Business Insider*, See's Candies has returned over 8000% since it was purchased back in 1972: Mohamed, Theron. "Warren Buffett's Favorite Business Is a Little Chocolate Maker with an 8000% Return. Here Are 5 Reasons Why He Loves See's Candies." *Markets Insider*, markets.businessinsider.com/news/stocks/warren-buffett-berkshire-hathaway-dream-business-is-sees-candies-2019-7-1029916323#a-return-of-8000-1. Accessed 6 Aug. 2022.

In fact, one time, a later CEO of the business attempted to stop selling 14 of the company's products keep the product line at about 100 items: "Chairman's Letter - 1987." Www.berkshirehathaway.com, www.berkshirehathaway.com/letters/1987.html. Accessed 10 Mar. 2022.

We put $25 million into it and it's given us over $2 billion of pretax income, well over $2 billion: Mohamed, Theron. "Warren Buffett's Favorite Business Is a Little Chocolate Maker with an 8000% Return. Here Are 5 Reasons Why He Loves See's Candies." *Markets Insider*, markets.businessinsider.com/news/stocks/warren-buffett-berkshire-hathaway-dream-business-is-sees-candies-2019-7-1029916323#a-return-of-8000-1. Accessed 6 Aug. 2022.

The reason that he [Elon Musk] is successful is because he doesn't get stuck down there. Because if he felt the need to micromanage each and every part on a Tesla... it would be very unlikely that he would have the capacity to do all that: "Elon Musk: A Leadership Case Study | Jocko Willink and Lex Fridman." *Www.youtube.com*, www.youtube.com/watch?v=ISSnxPk0Fn4&t=602s. Accessed 13 Aug. 2022.

According to Berkshire Hathaway's most recent annual report, Coca-Cola was purchased for about $1,299 million. As of the most recent annual filing, that investment is worth $23,684 million, producing incredible gains for Berkshire Hathaway: Berkshire Hathaway Inc. Form 10-K, https://www.berkshirehathaway.com/2021ar/2021ar.pdf.

He "liked the brand:" Antioco, John. "How I Did It: Blockbuster's Former CEO on Sparring with an Activist Shareholder." *Harvard Business Review*, Apr. 2011, hbr.org/2011/04/how-i-did-it-blockbusters-former-ceo-on-sparring-with-an-activist-shareholder.

At the same time, it only had 25% market share. This meant that 75% of the market wasn't owned by the company, indicating that there was a lot of potential to grow the company: Antioco, John. "How I Did It: Blockbuster's Former CEO on Sparring with an Activist Shareholder." *Harvard Business Review*, Apr. 2011, hbr.org/2011/04/how-i-did-it-blockbusters-former-ceo-on-sparring-with-an-activist-shareholder.

To date, Tesla has sold over 1.9 million electric vehicles: "How Many Teslas Have Been Sold? 25+ Tesla Car Sales Statistics." Fortunly, fortunly.com/statistics/tesla-car-sales-statistics/#gref.

Moreover, there were several small issues in the company that could be "fixed quickly," which could quickly boost profits for shareholders: Antioco, John. "How I Did It: Blockbuster's Former CEO on Sparring with an Activist Shareholder." *Harvard Business Review*, Apr. 2011, hbr.org/2011/04/how-i-did-it-blockbusters-former-ceo-on-sparring-with-an-activist-shareholder.

Tesla has over 50,000 employees: "LinkedIn Login, Sign in | LinkedIn." LinkedIn, 2022, www.linkedin.com/company/tesla-motors/people/?facetFieldOfStudy=101475.

Many people used to reason by analogy and tell Elon Musk that electric vehicle battery packs would always be too expensive at $600

per kilowatt hour: "The First Principles Method Explained by Elon Musk." YouTube, 4 Dec. 2013, www.youtube.com/watch?v=NV3sBlRgzTI.

According to the International Energy Agency, there were only 20,000 registered electric vehicles in the USA in 2011: "Global Sales and Sales Market Share of Electric Cars, 2010-2021 – Charts – Data & Statistics." IEA, www.iea.org/data-and-statistics/charts/global-sales-and-sales-market-share-of-electric-cars-2010-2021.

You can't say...'Nobody wants a car because horses are great and we're used to them and they can eat grass, there's lots of grass all over the place. And—you know—there's no gasoline that people can buy, so people are never going to get cars.' People did say that: "The First Principles Method Explained by Elon Musk." YouTube, 4 Dec. 2013, www.youtube.com/watch?v=NV3sBlRgzTI.

He "didn't believe that technology would threaten Blockbuster as fast as critics thought:" Antioco, John. "How I Did It: Blockbuster's Former CEO on Sparring with an Activist Shareholder." *Harvard Business Review*, Apr. 2011, hbr.org/2011/04/how-i-did-it-blockbusters-former-ceo-on-sparring-with-an-activist-shareholder.

Its inventory costs were too high at $65 per unit, preventing the company from being able to buy enough inventory to fulfill demand. So, to reduce inventory costs, Antioco formed a revenue sharing agreement with its suppliers. Under the agreement, the company only had to pay $1 per unit, but it had to give 40% of its revenues to its suppliers in return. Although it had to give away 40% of its sales, it was able to fulfill a larger portion of consumer demand because it could buy more inventory at $1 per unit than it could at $65 per unit: Antioco, John. 'How I Did It: Blockbuster's Former CEO on Sparring with an Activist Shareholder." *Harvard Business Review*, Apr. 2011, hbr.org/2011/04/how-i-did-it-blockbusters-former-ceo-on-sparring-with-an-activist-shareholder.

After leaving the company in 2007, Antioco sold all his Blockbuster stock and bought into Netflix at $20 per share because he "could see that Netflix was going to have the whole DVD-by-mail market handed to it:" Antioco, John. "How I Did It: Blockbuster's Former CEO on Sparring with an Activist Shareholder." *Harvard Business Review*, Apr. 2011, hbr.org/2011/04/how-i-did-it-blockbusters-former-ceo-on-sparring-with-an-activist-shareholder.

**"A specific way of thinking, based on the idea that because two or more things are similar in some respects, they are probably also similar in some further respect:" Küpers, Wendelin. "Analogical Reasoning." *Encyclopedia of the Sciences of Learning*, 2012, pp. 222–25, https://doi.org/10.1007/978-1-4419-1428-6_788.

The new supplier agreement contributed towards revenue growing from $4.4 billion: SECURITIES and EXCHANGE COMMISSION FORM 10-K Annual Report pursuant to Section 13 and 15(D). pdf.secdatabase.com/1077/0000930661-02-000951.pdf.

to $5.9 billion between 1999 and 2003: "BLOCKBUSTER INC (Form Type: 10-K, Filing Date: 03/15/2004)." *Edgar.secdatabase.com*, edgar.secdatabase.com/2406/119312504041361/filing-main.htm. Accessed 6 Aug. 2022.

Before joining Blockbuster, Antioco was the CEO of Taco Bell for just eight months, where he was tasked with turning around the company's streak of declining sales: Eben Shapiro and Nikhil Deogun Staff Reporters of the *Wall Street Journal*. "Antioco to Take Top Job at Troubled Blockbuster." *Wall Street Journal*, 4 June 1997, www.wsj.com/articles/SB865341927658260500.

Apple created a product that's now in the hands of over 1 billion consumers: Dean, Brian. "iPhone Users and Sales Stats for 2021." *Backlinko*, 28 May 2021, backlinko.com/iphone-users.

Coca-Cola tapped such a large market that consumers use 63 billion servings of either Coca-Cola's or another company's drinks every day: Washington, D. *UNITED STATES SECURITIES and EXCHANGE COMMISSION*. investors.coca-colacompany.com/filings-reports/annual-filings-10-k/content/0000021344-22-000009/0000021344-22-000009.pdf.

If you can focus obsessively enough on customer experience—selection, ease of use, low prices, more information to make purchase decisions with—if you can give customers all of that... then I think you have a good chance [at succeeding]: "Jeff Bezos 1999 Interview on Amazon before the Dotcom Bubble Burst." *CNBC*, 8 Feb. 2019, www.cnbc.com/video/2019/02/08/jeff-bezos-1999-interview-on-amazon-before-dotcom-bubble-burst.html.

In JCPenney's Q4 2012 earnings call, Ron Johnson didn't use the term EBITDA. But did that make him a good manager? No. His turnaround strategy destroyed the company's sales: "J.C. Penney (JCP) Q2 2017 Results - Earnings Call Transcript | Seeking Alpha." *Seekingalpha.com*, seekingalpha.com/article/4098095-j-c-penney-jcp-q2-2017-results-earnings-call-transcript. Accessed 6 Aug. 2022.

What matters is the pace of innovation. That is the fundamental determinant of competitiveness of any given company.... This is obvious that this would occur with Amazon and Walmart because Walmart's rate of innovation was negligible, and Amazon's was very high. The outcome was obvious a long time ago: "Elon Musk Destroys Stupid Investment Bankers and Makes Fun of Daimler CEO." *Www.youtube.com*, www.youtube.com/watch?v=HxAoQSkMHcw&t=24s. Accessed 6 Aug. 2022.

THE 5-MINUTE RUBRIC

In fact, a source that calls itself the "one stop solution to financial inquiries" states that it should only take 2-4 hours to research a company: "How Much Time Should I Spend Researching Stocks?" *App.fintrakk.com*, app.fintrakk.com/article/how-much-time-should-i-spend-researching-stocks. Accessed 6 Aug. 2022.

One popular value investing fund, Ariel Investments, is quite detailed with its research. They typically have their analysts write "full-blown" research reports, conduct balance sheet analyses, valuation analyses, and competitive analyses. They have several portfolio management teams look at every stock several times, allowing them to get a diverse set of perspectives. They have a dedicated "devil's advocate" to challenge the current consensus. They talk with management teams to understand a firm's strengths and weaknesses. In the end, they may end up spending "several months" analyzing a stock: Rogers, J. (n.d.). *Investing with a Patient, Long-Term View* (ticker, Interviewer) [Review of *Investing with a Patient, Long-Term View*]. Retrieved August 6, 2022, from https://www.arielinvestments.com/images/stories/Articles/2017/2017-ticker-investing-with-patient-long-term-view.pdf

Though I had never heard of Larson-Juhl before Craig's call, a few minutes' talk with him made me think we would strike a deal. He was straightforward in describing the business, cared about who bought it, and was realistic as to price. Two days later, Craig and Steve McKenzie, his CEO, came to Omaha and in ninety minutes we reached an agreement: Berkshire Hathaway Inc. Form 10-K, https://www.berkshirehathaway.com/2001ar/2001ar.pdf.

Jack Ringwalt, a friend of mine who was the controlling shareholder of the two companies, came to my office saying he would like to sell. Fifteen minutes later, we had a deal: Berkshire Hathaway Inc. Form 10-K, https://www.berkshirehathaway.com/2014ar/2014ar.pdf.

We can promise complete confidentiality and a very fast answer—customarily within five minutes—as to whether we're interested: Berkshire Hathaway Inc. Form 10-K, https://www.berkshirehathaway.com/2017ar/2017ar.pdf.

We have a bunch of filters [Rubrics] we've developed in our minds over time.... So, we really can tell you in five minutes whether we're interested in [a business]: "Collection: Warren Buffett - #58 Investing 'the 5 Minutes Test.'" *Www.youtube.com*, www.youtube.com/watch?v=nmyok42DQHk&t=326s. Accessed 6 Aug. 2022.

And now, what many young graduates and also more inexperienced business professionals will do is that they will say, 'Until I have closed [the] gaps, until I've really looked at everything, until I've really done my thorough research, no way I can come up with a solution. Until I did all of this, right?' And this, my friends, is not how you should operate in the business world: "HOW TO SOLVE PROBLEMS - How Do Consulting Firms Work (Hypothesis-Based Problem Solving Explained)." Www.youtube.com, www.youtube.com/watch?v=TBvJzXxRuxs&t=571s. Accessed 18 Aug. 2022.

Let me give you a simple example that was created by Heinrich Rusche. Let's say that there is a hypothetical payment service provider that is looking to expand into the Brazilian market: "HOW TO SOLVE PROBLEMS - How Do Consulting Firms Work (Hypothesis-Based Problem Solving Explained)." Www.youtube.com, www.youtube.com/watch?v=TBvJzXxRuxs&t=571s. Accessed 18 Aug. 2022.

That caught some people off guard. It made people ask themselves, "can Warren Buffett really make investment decisions that quickly?:" "Collection: Warren Buffett - #58 Investing 'the 5 Minutes Test.'" Www.youtube.com, www.youtube.com/watch?v=nmyok42DQHk&t=227s.

In the annual report, you stated that 'if anyone out there has a good company, like FlightSafety, please let you know, and you'd be glad to look it over and give an answer within five minutes or less'...How can [you] do that?: "Collection: Warren Buffett - #58 Investing 'the 5 Minutes Test.'" Www.youtube.com, www.youtube.com/watch?v=nmyok42DQHk&t=227s.

They have 40 or so training centers around the world—I'd never set foot in one of them. I'd never been to their headquarters.... I think most of the people in this room, if they just focused on what made a good business or didn't make a good business, and thought about it for a little while, they could develop a set of filters that would let them, in five minutes, figure out pretty well what made sense and or didn't make sense: "Collection: Warren Buffett - #58 Investing 'the 5 Minutes Test.'" Www.youtube.com, www.youtube.com/watch?v=nmyok-42DQHk&t=227s.

I've nothing to add except that people underrate the importance of a few simple big ideas.... A few big ideas really work: "Collection: Warren Buffett - #58 Investing 'the 5 Minutes Test.'" Www.youtube.com, www.youtube.com/watch?v=nmyok42DQHk&t=227s.

From very early on, whenever I took a position in the markets, I wrote down the criteria I used to make my decision: Dalio, Ray. "My Road of Trials." *Principles: Life and Work*. Simon & Schuster, 2017, pp. 32-35.

From very early on, whenever I took a position in the markets, I wrote down the criteria I used to make my decision. Then, when I closed out a trade, I could reflect on how well these criteria had worked. It occurred to me that if I wrote those criteria into formulas (now more fashionably called algorithms) and then ran historical data through them, I could test how well my rules would have worked in the past.... And [then] modify the decision rules appropriately: Dalio, Ray. "My Road of Trials." *Principles: Life and Work*. Simon & Schuster, 2017, pp. 32-35.

Well, I was lucky. I had a sensational teacher, Ben Graham.... Ben made it terribly interesting, because we walked into that class and we valued companies. And he had various little games he would play with us. Sometimes he would have us evaluate company A and company B with a whole bunch of figures, and then we would find out that A and B were the same company at different points in its history, for example.... There were a lot of little games he played to get us to think about the key variables and how we could go off the track: "How Warren Buffett Would Teach Investing [Collection: Warren Buffett]." Www.youtube.com, www.youtube.com/watch?v=x1XGdhVTGK8. Accessed 18 Aug. 2022.

THE FRAMEWORK

To invest successfully over a lifetime does not require a stratospheric IQ, unusual business insights, or inside information. What's needed is a sound intellectual framework for making decisions and the ability to keep emotions from corroding that framework: Maxfield, John. "A Sound Intellectual Framework for Investors." The Motley Fool, 27

Aug. 2013, www.fool.com/investing/general/2013/08/27/a-sound-intellec-tual-framework-for-investors.aspx#:~:text=Warren%20Buffett%2C%20 the%20greatest%20investor.

A framework is simply "a particular set of rules, ideas, or beliefs which you use in order to deal with problems or to decide what to do:" Collins English Dictionary | Definitions, Translations, Example Sentences and Pronunciations." *Collinsdictionary.com*, 25 Oct. 2019, www.collinsdictionary.com/us/dictionary/english.

Made in United States
Orlando, FL
07 March 2023